Time Out of Mind

A Love Story:
An Involuntary Experience
of Altered Perception

Jo Thomas

authorHOUSE®

AuthorHouse™ UK
1663 Liberty Drive
Bloomington, IN 47403 USA
www.authorhouse.co.uk
Phone: 0800.197.4150

© 2017 Jo Thomas. All rights reserved.
Cover credit from a painting by the author.

No part of this book may be reproduced, stored in a retrieval system, or transmitted by any means without the written permission of the author.

This account is based on actual occurrences. Although names have been changed for reasons of privacy, apart from Tom and Jo, it must be regarded as a truthful statement.

Published by AuthorHouse 02/16/2017

ISBN: 978-1-5246-7805-0 (sc)
ISBN: 978-1-5246-7806-7 (hc)
ISBN: 978-1-5246-7807-4 (e)

Print information available on the last page.

Any people depicted in stock imagery provided by Thinkstock are models, and such images are being used for illustrative purposes only.
Certain stock imagery © Thinkstock.

This book is printed on acid-free paper.

Because of the dynamic nature of the Internet, any web addresses or links contained in this book may have changed since publication and may no longer be valid. The views expressed in this work are solely those of the author and do not necessarily reflect the views of the publisher, and the publisher hereby disclaims any responsibility for them.

Contents

Foreword xi
Introduction 1
Prelude 3
Fugue 47
Coda 153
Rest 175
Afterthoughts 177

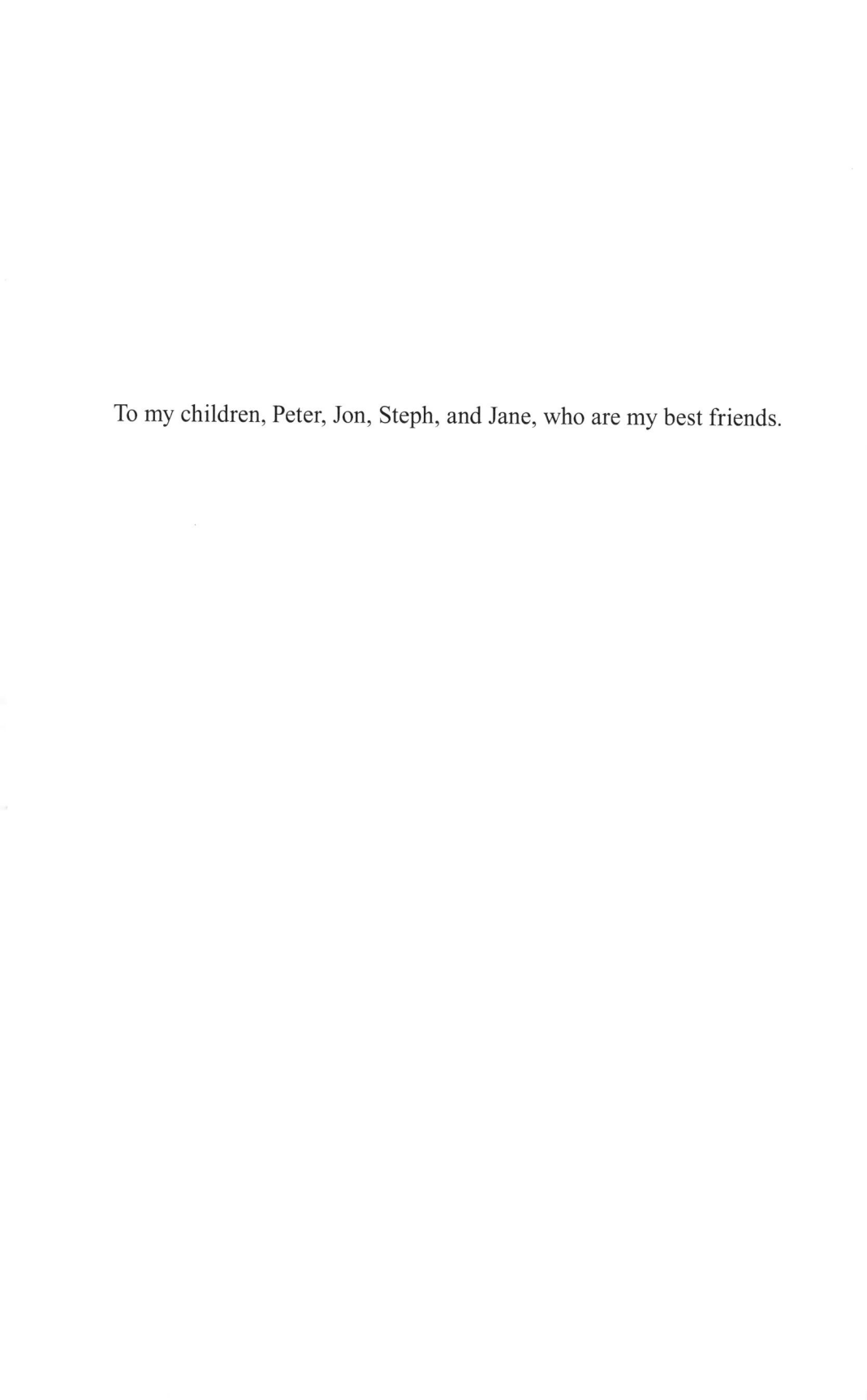

To my children, Peter, Jon, Steph, and Jane, who are my best friends.

Acknowledgements

I am immensely grateful to my children and my own family, who showed extraordinary patience and loyalty when I was behaving in ways none of us could fully understand; to Tom Barnard, who gave essential help with preparing the work for printing with computer technology; Amy Stanton, who typed out the first version on an ancient typewriter; and Fred Turner, who offered huge encouragement and support throughout this whole story.

Foreword

I am one of the friends – the poet – that Jo mentions in this extraordinary book. I am also her nephew and know many of the people she describes. So I am qualified to vouch for the absolute honesty of her account and for its truth to external fact. Of course I can't testify as to the terrifying, agonizing, and beautiful worlds she traverses on the inside. But I was with her through some of it, and I believe the great clarity and wise innocence of her nature is testimony enough to its truth.

Jo Harding has offered us a path into a region that deeply scares us, because it is there in ourselves, for the most part safely penned up in our dreams and forgotten every morning. Like Theseus – a figure she follows into the labyrinth of the human mind – she meets her minotaur, and is able, using her unwound clue of meditation, to return safely to the world of human community. But unlike Theseus, she does not slay the minotaur. She somehow tames him for human purposes and uses his strength to release her and to propel her poetry to create a future that has proved to be hugely productive of art, music, and family life.

I believe the full experiences of falling in love and being in love are much rarer than is claimed. Of course all of us have felt that physical and spiritual glow of huge attraction to another person, as valid for other animals as it is for us. But love of Jo's sort – the incredible luck of finding the true soulmate – is something different. And to lose that in the midst of its full celebration is almost unimaginably terrible. What could be worse? Hell? The torments of hell are, by Dante's admission, only an image, an allegory, a metaphor, of that grief.

Jo has walked in that dreadful terrain and come back to tell the tale. To walk it, she convinces me, requires a sojourn in true madness (or should one say 'shamanic ordeal' or mystical 'sparagmos'– being torn limb from limb? Indeed, there is a moment when part of her is literally torn away).

"O the mind, mind has mountains, cliffs of fall, frightful, sheer, no-man-fathomed. Hold them cheap may who ne'er hung there" says Gerard Manley Hopkins. If we think we can get through that place without going mad, we are deceiving ourselves. And if we do come back, and heal ourselves as she healed herself, we become healers ourselves, healers of great power.

This book is part of the medicine she has been offering to all her friends and relatives ever since, a beneficial potion for many, and a secret source of our extended family's achievements and rescues. Her imagination has, for instance, been an essential part of my own poetic work and a vital thread in my philosophical journey.

To achieve her victory – the triumph of irrepressible joy over despair and pain – she had to show a heroic temperament and call on a remarkable stubborn vitality. In her nineties now, she still has a trace of that amazing physical vigour she had when she was a young mother. She was physically very strong, quick, graceful in an entirely unstudied way, unconsciously beautiful, with the ample bosom of the Davises and the good bones of the Howards, her forebears. She was passionate and commonsensical at the same time, full of compassion, a bit careless and always ready for conversation. A hero.

Her huge courage is shown in this book by her unflinching willingness to deal with the sexual side of 'madness', and in the most intimate way. Even in very good accounts of that journey, like Greenberg's *I Never Promised You a Rose Garden*, the false social shame of sexuality when combined with madness has been a taboo subject. Certainly Cole Porter's lines, "In olden days, a glimpse of stocking was looked on as something shocking; now, God knows, anything goes", indicate a change from the almost Victorian atmosphere of Jo's childhood.

We have been gradually loosening the cruel bonds by which, as Blake says, religion and convention once spent their time "binding with briars [our] joys and desires". (And we have often trivialized the joys and desires in the process.) But the *combination* of sexuality and madness is still deeply disturbing. We don't want to go there. Freud had the courage to do so, but he deals with the psyche, not the soul, with neurosis but not shamanic possession, the Id but not the spirit as expressed in the flesh. Schizophrenia is a label, not an explanation. Any good explanation must come from the inside, and that is what Jo Harding provides.

And it is here that a great potential lies for healing. Much madness is divinest sense, says Emily Dickinson. And the madness that dare not say its name, the sexual kind, needs to be recognized if we are to fully encounter the healing of our humanity (especially our female humanity).

Only the innocence and blazing goodness of a person like Jo could undertake this task, this pharmakon for the wounded snake of our nature. Torn away from the person to whom she had given herself as the source of life, her unfulfilled desire for him propels her on her journey into enlightenment and peace.

That desire also inspires Jo's remarkable poetry, which ranges in form from a free verse of dense rich symbolism and violent feeling to formal measures that show a truly literate mind at work, setting into a beautiful shape material that comes from the stark edge of our human experience. Her wordplay reflects the synchronicity of her vision – the sound of words, their flesh, is not a mere passive vessel of their meaning, but an active demonstration of the deep patterns that lie below quotidian existence. Her poetry makes chronos into kairos, endurance into epiphany.

A word about Tom, her husband-lover, my uncle, the father of her children, my cousins. Tom was one of my greatest teachers. I learned more philosophy from him than from anyone else in my life. And all the time I argued with him fiercely, and he was always gentle and patient and good-humoured with my teenage intellectual arrogance. Jo was not deceived by him: he was all she says he was. His goodness – though utterly empirical and rational – was full kin to hers.

—Frederick Turner

Introduction

Insanity – madness – would not seem to be a likely subject for a love story, nor would it be something to do with our relationship with God. It turns out to be both.

This is an eyewitness account of my own experience of a journey into the mysterious world of an altered perception not induced by drugs or any stimulus other than the desire for reunion with the beloved 'other' ... Eurydice rather than Orpheus searching the underworld.

Mental illness still tends to be taboo. It has not often been described by the one who experiences it but more often as a case history, or as a subject for analysis. Something that happens to someone else.

Two people from totally different backgrounds meet in 1949. They experience poverty, homelessness, social change in the '50s, and emerge victorious from their struggles. Suddenly the man dies, aged forty-four, leaving his wife with four children, when the youngest was two years old.

My journey to wholeness explored the labyrinth of madness, a loss of meaning which was further exacerbated in the setting of psychiatric hospitals.

During these episodes I was aware of deeper levels of human history, which emerged unbidden, vividly 'remembered', retold as they occurred in the context of the events described. Fantasy? As always with every fiction, some sharp shards of truth pierce the web. The poems, placed as illustrations in the text, were written at the time of the experience, when other ways to communicate were blocked.

Fifty years ago, when this record begins, there were but few authors writing about the inner worlds of our human experience. In recent decades there has been a magnificent proliferation of such themes.

Introduction

Reading them, I feel that my anguish of feeling, as I unwittingly explored my own depths, seems curiously out of date! Maybe there are others out there who also were caught in a web of misunderstanding and felt imperilled; perhaps in revealing my version of 'doing madness', others my find some hope and healing, and the opposites become reconciled.

Prelude

The Elixer
A man that looks on glass
On it may stay his eye
Or if he pleases, through it pass
And then the heavens espy
George Herbert

August 1949

I had just arrived at summer school. We were going to study politics, review the world and its pains, and seek remedies. People arrived with their cases and went to find their allotted rooms, a mild excitement in their eyes as they observed the faces of the others, some old friends and the possibility of new ones. It was a fine day in early August, the fourth.

Thirty-five years before, a great war had just begun; another one had just finished. We were hopeful, idealistic. Possibilities teased us like the distant summit of a mountain peak viewed at the beginning of a summer holiday, the resolve already formed to climb it and see beyond.

I put my case under my bed, hung up some dresses, and noted my roommates. I was a schoolteacher, and I had that spacious feeling that comes of knowing there was still a month before the next term started. There was an hour yet before supper, and I could hear laughter in the garden below. I ran out to look and was at once beckoned to a game of volleyball with four or five people on each side of the net. I began to enjoy myself. I was twenty-four and had a lively body. I had never slept with a man. I had thought myself in love a couple of times but just decided I would not trouble my heart with hopes of marriage for a while. People around me seemed always in some anguish from the experience of being in love, and I had just been rejected yet again. It seemed better to leave it all alone and be free. Perhaps it would come later, especially if I stopped trying so hard. So I joined in the game, leaping about and laughing, glad to be there and not expecting to win.

Breathless, we paused for a moment between games and flung ourselves on the grass. I looked at the house above us on a bank and saw it had a long conservatory within filled with tables and chairs. Glass panels came right down to the floor, and it was easy to see what lay beyond.

Two men were sitting in wicker armchairs, talking. They were facing each other, and I could see their profiles. Suddenly, the one on the left turned his head, and it seemed as if he looked straight at me. He wore a blue shirt without a tie, and I could see even from that distance that his eyes were blue. He had very curly, dark brown hair, rather untidy, and a broad brow. I couldn't take my eyes away from this face, and it was a long time before I realised I was staring at him. I knew he must have been looking at me in the same way. I came out of this rather more like arousing from a sleep than from a wakeful state of mind. I had completely stopped thinking while his gaze was on me.

He looked away and began to talk to his friends again, and I got up to rejoin the volleyball game. A single clear thought came through and bypassed everything else I was doing, and it was undeniable. There could be no resistance. This man, whom I had never seen before and had not yet spoken to, was going to be my husband.

"This is silly", I retorted to myself.

Not so, came the reply. *You're going to marry him.*

"But why him?"

You'll understand later.

I'd never had such a curious encounter with my own mind. It was like another person speaking from a great depth inside. Some minutes later, the face that had been behind the glass was looking at me from the other side of the net. He was taller than I was and looked strong.

After the game was over, we all stood around, talking. His eyes were indeed a very dark blue and warm in their depths. I had forgotten to ask his name, so I looked at the notice board on the way to supper to see if any of the ones on the room list looked as if it could belong to him. The first one I read was one I liked – Tom – and he was a coal miner from South Wales. Yes, that could be right. He had a slight lilt of Welsh when he spoke.

After supper, about thirty people, quite a mixture of ages and backgrounds, got together in the largest room, which served as a lecture hall and social common room. Someone had provided a gramophone with a few records of dance music. It was all a bit makeshift, but everyone was cheerful and ready to join hands when the Paul Jones started. This was supposed to bring everyone together. The girls formed a circle on the inside and the men on the outside. Running in opposite directions, one would end up opposite a partner when the music stopped. The running seemed more exuberant than usual, and hands were pulling the circles more and more rapidly to the strident notes of the little hand-wound gramophone.

The circles fell apart, like the chain falling off a bike. My hands jerked out of the one next to me, and I stumbled over, hitting my forehead, bone on bone, against the side of someone's head. It was the man I had seen that afternoon. I rebounded backwards and fell flat on my back. For a few seconds I was once again in that peculiar state where one can observe one's own doings and feelings from a detached, silent awareness. What I saw were stars – beautifully coloured flowers of light floating around just above eyes, which looked out and saw only blackness. The stars floated in and out of the velvet background. I came round and found myself being pulled up by my assailant. He had warm, firm hands, and they made me feel I would not fall ever again. I touched my forehead to see if it was swelling. I felt no pain.

"All right", I said, "let's dance then!"

He looked concerned. "Hadn't you better sit down?"

"No, please, I want to dance this. I'm not very good at ballroom stuff, though I think it's a waltz".

He confessed that he didn't know how to do it either, and we spent the next five minutes working hard at not tripping each other until the circles were formed again for a reshuffle of pairs. Good. We were back together again. Another clumsy attempt at putting feet in the right places. This time we gave up, laughing at our hopeless failures to get it right.

He asked me to walk along the lane to cool off. It led downhill towards the town. We could see the flickering lights on the seafront, and a warm wind blew in a salty smell. In half an hour we had exchanged most of the basic facts about ourselves – our ages, jobs, and quite a lot about our families and ways of life.

We walked under the neon lights and then into the darker places between them, where the trees bent low over the road. We stopped for quite a time, still talking. I felt light, a little breathless, a thin, delicate, and warm feeling enfolding the words as they flowed, patterning the breath with sounds. The lightness was like a release of the gravity that binds our feet to the ground; I could have floated up. I had dreams of this several times before. In them I was wafted like a seed head a few inches above the meadow grass. It was not a truly physical feeling; my body did not appear to be involved. I heard his words, and I answered him. But at the same time, I felt that something of us both became detached and joined beyond the fact of these two people standing in the road.

Coal miner, working class, eldest of five. Left school at 14 to work in the steelworks and then the war and the army in India and Malaya. Read a lot of books because he lived in a street next to a library. Father a carpenter, mother a cook.

Schoolteacher; middle class, youngest of eight. Father and mother missionaries in India; father now a retired GP. Had been religious, but not now. Music (singing in chorus), painting, and politics.

It didn't seem much to go on, worlds apart even but for the war and its effects of equalising the different sections of community life. I'd been to a private boarding school run by a missionary-type woman. Tom had passed for the grammar school but had to leave and earn his living when the family got broke.

The strange feeling remained while we walked back. I didn't know what he felt but knew without speech that we were meant to be together, and time and space had nothing to do with it.

I went to the dormitory and got into bed. I didn't sleep but lay afloat on a lightness, as if I were a cirrus cloud high over a grassy down. I did not think of him so much as be aware of him. I was enfolded by something which was his as flower petals enfold the fragile pollen, all one. No excitement, but the centre of my body above the diaphragm was expanded by a glow of warmth. Gradually, it got light outside, and the trees went from grey to green as the sun rose.

I got up very quietly so as not to wake the others and went out barefoot down to the lawn where we had played volleyball. The dewy grass gently tickled the soles of my feet. My mind very awake and full, I was aware of a supreme silence, a quietness inside myself.

A couple of days passed, and each evening Tom walked with me as we exchanged in more detail our respective lives. During classes through the days I found his face and mine turned towards each other.

On the third day there was an afternoon of free time. He took my arm and led me to the garden, where there was a stile leading to the meadows.

"Let's go there; we can be alone".

As I walked beside him I found myself saying yes. I said yes several times in answer to some question not asked. I said it to myself and to him and could not have unsaid it. "Yes, yes, yes".

He looked at me, not surprised but laughing a little. There were some sheep in the first field, and in the next some geese wandered in a squawking line down to a pond. We found ourselves in a fold of the valley, concealed from every side. The sweet grass of late summer stood high, with marguerites and scarlet pimpernels, lady-smock and a lark in the warm blue above.

We sat down without a word. He picked some flowers and laid them in my lap. For a long time he looked at me, and I looked back. Then he took my hands and held them, not moving. It was a slow, healing warmth, and something akin to a ripening. The yeast in the dough changing its texture, a supreme alteration of value. The kiss that followed was not so much an expression of desire, not a sexual embrace. It was an overflowing; the joy brimmed up and spilled out gently, filling every crevice of body and mind; not asking or answering, not even an exchange. It was not two people but one, with the grass, the bird, the sky, the warm wind blowing. Nothing to say or explain. We stood up, hand in hand, a vast sense of ease, effortless and free, knowing each other.

Prelude

Next day a letter came. Tom would be leaving early – an interview for a place in a College of Further Education in North Wales. I sat on the grass verge with him while he waited for the bus, and I gave him my address in case he wanted to write and tell me if he got accepted. He left. My mind went with him. I started a letter. It was more like an essay. I filled many pages and I've no idea what I wrote. I was still writing it three days later when a letter came from him. I took it, unopened, down to the beach, and sat looking at it for a long time. Then I opened it, very slowly, and the words all blurred together because tears came to my eyes even before I'd read anything. The ink was blue, the writing straightforward, flowing with long even strokes up and down.

It said, simply, "We could get married. Come to South Wales. We'll find somewhere to live; get a tent even".

There was a little more; it didn't matter. I wrote back and said, "Yes, I will".

Only six days altogether and I was sure, so sure. Nothing to go on but an effervescent trust. We had no savings, no premiums, no insurances. We had not slept together (I was, in fact, a virgin!). What kind of thing *was* this? It wasn't at all what was expected of me; my reason did not hear nor make a judgement. The joy shouted aloud in my head flooding it with light. I was laughing and crying at the same time when I read his letter, and all I could think or say was yes.

I turned to look at my sister and her three young children, who were sitting on the pebbles beside me. The August sun was hot, and there was a beach smell of sea and sweat and salt. The waves at our feet dissolved into the sand between the pebbles, and I still couldn't see in focus because of the tears.

I needed no thought, no deliberate plan. Everything was clear and very simple. I said, "This coal miner I met – he wants me to marry him. I'll go to Wales to see him and give my notice at my job".

Two weeks later I was in the train arriving at Cardiff Station. It was my first sight of the place, and I felt a stranger as I went down the steps to the subway and along the arched passage to the exit I wondered what his face was like, really; I could remember it, but it suddenly seemed a very long way off. What would I feel? Had I been so right or was it all an illusion? That shape of truth lost its defined edge for a moment.

Time Out of Mind

I came through the barrier, and he was there, standing alone, wearing an old tweed jacket and an open-neck shirt, a little above average height for a Welshman; he smiled. At once I felt strange, sharp sensation in my chest at the base of my lungs – a piercing sweetness, almost a pain. He put my arm under his, holding my right hand, took my case, and led me to a bus. I didn't see the streets at all on the way to his parents' home. He told me I would spend a night there and then we would go to the Wye Valley for a few days.

The house was in a side street, had a small terrace, and seemed dark inside. His mother welcomed me with a smile that shined on a face that showed weariness and pain. She had lustrous green-blue eyes and a large aching body, legs giving way in huge varicose veins, the result of overlong standing in her job as cook in a big hotel in the centre of the town.

Later, his two schoolgirl sisters appeared, lively and whispering together like sparrows in the early morning, glancing at me with some curiosity, but accepting me without question.

His father came last, a burly man, not tall, with a broad head, the bald crown covered by a large and ancient hat. He spoke loudly, but the tone was gentle, and he sat down at once to eat the heaped plate of food handed him by his wife. No ceremony or polite behaviour. A natural easiness and acceptance of my being there.

I sat on the sofa in the back room which served as everyone's resting place and took in the atmosphere. It was untidy; everything was old, paint peeling off walls and ceiling, clothes and papers lying in corners. The room felt warm and welcoming. No pressure or anticipation of how I would react in these surroundings. I was always being criticised for being untidy at home, so I was relaxed and grateful for this mellow muddle.

I got into bed in a tiny box room. Much later on (I was not asleep) my future husband came softly in and lay beside me on the bed. We embraced silently, and he left me after a little while, promising that we should share a bed all night before very long. That seemed a very beautiful prospect, to be asleep with him. To pass into that nothingness, oblivion, with my arms around him and his strength melted into mine.

We set out with a rucksack on the bus to Chepstow. We sat on the top deck and soaked up the sunshine and each other's laughter. He

Prelude

discovered that he could make me squeak if he squeezed my leg just above the knee. He put my hand into his pocket and held it there, gently massaging my fingers. We bought food in Chepstow and set out up the valley road.

By dusk we had arrived at Tintern, passing the abbey after a long walk through the trees of the valley, glimpsing the gleam of Wye water between. We walked to the far side of the village and came to the tiny railway halt on the bend of the river. It was nearly dark, and a sliver of moon was rising above Offa's Dyke on the far side of the valley. We sat on the bench of the little wooden shelter by the one-track railway and ate bread and cheese and a few tomatoes. The bench was a long one, so we lay down to sleep on it end to end, with our heads touching.

Around four in the morning we decided that narrow wooden benches were not meant for sleeping on and moved off across the road into a meadow which sloped up towards the trees of Tintern Forest. Venus hung a visible crescent in the southern sky. We lay on Tom's raincoat and put mine over the top, side by side this time. The star shined a silent blessing, and this became our nuptial rite. An initiation, a beginning. The promise given and received. We had a lot to learn.

Around seven we got up and walked on, past Brockweir Bridge and beside the forest towards Llandogo. We slipped off the road for a while and lay on the soft floor of the pine wood and sought the matching of ourselves.

Still a little unfamiliar with my own body in this new role, I told him, as we slid down the slope, my bare backside scratching into the pine needles, "Rolling down this hill is one way to take your woman. What I really want is to get into a proper bed with you".

Llandogo was the next place on the road. The valley broadens there, wide water meadows where scouts were camping. We saw a sign and walked up to a wooden bungalow bed and breakfast, set well back from the road and needing a coat of paint. We booked for a couple of nights and gave our name as Mr and Mrs. I kept my left hand out of sight in case she spotted that I had no ring yet.

We spent the rest of the day walking around the valley, over Bigsweir Bridge, up the hill to St Briaevels, rejoicing in the warm sun and the benevolence of the woods and hills, the swift river with its swinging curves. Then to the village in the soft dusk, a quiet supper of home-made pie and garden vegetables.

The lady was motherly and seemed to guess we were newlyweds. She showed us our room, very plain and simple, a cotton quilt over the brass bedstead, a big bolster instead of pillows. No electricity here, only a candle. Tom was already in bed when I returned from getting a wash. I'd put a nightdress on, feeling suddenly modest. I took it off as soon as I was under the quilt and then lost myself forever in the effulgence of his radiant body – he wearing mine like a robe of stars in the Milky Way. I got my wish then to sleep with him. Folded together we slept and dreamed, turned together, breathed softly the same air, kindness incarnate, fire of love – a tiny flame burning in a windless place.

Early next morning we woke. From a thin wooden partition from across the passage we heard a voice – a woman's plaintive, half angry, half pleading, "Why don't you do like other men? Other husbands get up and go to work. Why don't you get up then! I always have to drag you out. Get up, you lazy dog, like other women's husbands do".

We lay very still and listened, a little shocked to overhear these private words. Tom put his mouth close to my ear. "Jo, is that what you will say to me when you get me up to go to work?"

I giggled and lay on my back. We were man and woman, and we were one flesh. His arm, flung over me, felt as if it had melted into my bosom. This one night of sleep had fused us, wedded us. The old brass bedstead had joined us in matrimony, and it felt altogether holy – not mystical but wholesome, like a loaf of bread freshly baked.

There was home-made bread for breakfast. We went out, across the village high street and into the meadows where the river ran, swift brown currents curling into the banks, cutting under at the muddy corners where the cows would trample their way to the water. We walked not talking much, for we were content, eased by our weddedness. We set out alongside the little rail track, following it downstream by the riverbank.

Eventually, we reached a shack, a tiny halt for the single carriage diesel train. A passing cloud dropped a little rain, and we sat on the wooden bench, listening to the rain clattering on the corrugated iron roof. Suddenly, with no warning at all, I felt a vast sorrow. A deep tearing sadness clamped itself in my whole body. The sharpness of it took away my breath but only lasted a few seconds. When it passed I found that I was crying, gently, without noise.

Tom turned towards me and saw my face. He found a handkerchief and wiped my eyes, held my face in his hands. "Why?" he asked.

"I don't know – I don't in the least know".

The tears came again, and he dried them.

"It's something to do with us. I feel you're not always going to be here; you might have to go away, a long way away. I trust you absolutely. Perhaps I'm like the Red Queen in *Alice in Wonderland*. She always screamed before she was hurt. It's all right, Tom. This feeling is going away now; it will soon pass!"

I had never felt such a thing before, such an abstract grief. It didn't make sense, and Tom took off his jacket and put it round me as I was cold and trembling. He held me, and I put my head against his chest where I could hear his heart beating.

The clouds broke apart and let the sun through; the meadow gleamed and glistened; the cows looked as if they had been painted on it. We got up and went outside to the little wooden platform.

He didn't rebuke or question me. He trusted me. "I'm here", he said. "I'll always be here, and I will never leave you. It's fine – all fine".

I went back to my job at the girls grammar school, applied for another in South Wales and got it. We wrote to each other every day and snatched some weekends together. We planned to marry in a registry office around Christmas.

Meanwhile, Tom left his job at the pit in the small mining town of Ystrad Mynach. He lived in a miners hostel there and felt the need to be in Cardiff where we could find some rooms to live together. He got a temporary job as an income tax clerk.

My father and mother met him one weekend. Uncertain at first what to make of his lack of education, they liked his 'good Christian face' and accepted him. My father died of a stroke soon after this, and my mother felt disinclined to attend a civil marriage – she was a deeply religious woman and diffident of her role with Tom's family. So I packed my things and travelled down to Cardiff a few days before Christmas. On Christmas Eve we were wed.

It was a crisp bright morning and the office looked shabby as most offices were after the war had ended. We sat to wait our turn on a narrow wooden bench like the one on Tintern Station. A girl sat at a long typewriter which recorded the facts of our lives at great speed, and then Tom pushed the ring over my finger. His father and sister were witnesses; no one else was present. We both expected a quiet day. Our amazement was beyond telling when we got back to the house. A complete Christmas dinner awaited us, together with a vast four-tier cake and at least twenty people, new relatives I had never seen before. The front parlour was jammed tight with beaming faces and convivial Cardiff accents. Plenty of wine appeared, and my mother-in-law's cooking was unsurpassed even for her.

When the merriment died down a little and the food settled somewhat, we were ushered into the street where an old workmate of my new father had brought up his horse and cart. My boxes and bits were brought out and put on top. Tom and I climbed on, and we set off at brisk pace through the town. I had a bag of cold turkey which 'Mum' had thrust into my hand (we lived on it for almost a week) and soon arrived at our lodging – a couple of rooms in a pleasant tree-lined street in Roath.

So this was it. We were really and truly man and wife. Tom had become redundant a couple of weeks before and had spent his last few pounds on the ring.

The next few years went fast. We seemed to be always moving, looking for somewhere better to live. Tom had various jobs, but none were of real interest to him. He was the breadwinner. I gave up teaching a few weeks before the birth of our first son. Our landlady did not really want a baby in the house, and we were immensely relieved and grateful when a friend offered us the use of a cottage in the Vale of Gwent.

From now on our life was punctuated by moves. We had scarcely settled in a place when some undeniable occasion would arise and shift us off somewhere else. Tom worked in a glass works, as a builder's labourer, as a presser in a dry cleaners. He even tried his luck as a seller of *Encyclopaedia Britannica* but never got rid of a single set. He took Kleen-Eezy brushes from door to door, and on one occasion got a job as an inspector of engineering lathe operators in a small factory without having the least qualification for the job.

Our baby was thriving, and the three of us enjoyed our times together splendidly. We'd carry him on our shoulders up the Welsh hillsides, splash with him in the sea. We had to put up with lack of privacy and makeshift cooking arrangements in the places we lived in, but nothing could stop the wholeness that we all felt together. We moved from the Gwent cottage to share a house in the mining valley of Duffryn Rhondda. Here we were suddenly plagued with a family disaster.

I was not a good housewife. I took too much time with my little son; I played with him when I could have been keeping the place clean. I loved cooking but had no awareness of the mess I spread all around. One day I left the wash boiler on and it boiled over, flooded through to the floor below, and spoiled a newly decorated room. My landlady was enraged by my carelessness and let loose a flood of angry reproach against my chaotic housewifery and ordered us to leave at once. I wept, bitterly ashamed, not knowing what to do. I was expecting another baby, and we had nowhere to live.

Tom came home from the factory where he was working. I felt deeply reassured as soon as he arrived. My guilty feelings were justified enough, but he made me feel forgiven though he never said a word. Next day we walked over the mountain path to the next village, carrying 2-year-old Rueben on our shoulders, borrowed ten pounds off a friend Tom had met at a political meeting, and arranged to move our belongings back to Cardiff. We were given shelter for a few months by a couple who had a spare room. I discovered I was going to have twins, and our hosts gave up their own larger bedroom to us so I could sleep in a big bed with my man and have some space to put my enormous belly. We knew we couldn't stay there long – there would be five of us in one room. In any case, it was not for us to use our friends' space any longer than we could help.

The babies arrived, supremely healthy and very large. I felt so elated when they were born that I spent the first five minutes after their arrival laughing until the walls echoed. It was pure joy to be a mother again, and doubly so for two such magnificent sons.

I found I could feed them both again, as I had our Rueben; there was an overflowing abundance of milk for them, with enough left over for the premature babies downstairs. I brought the boys back to my friend's house, and then we started to plan our next move. Tom had a casual job painting girders and didn't mind what work he got. I decided to take the pram and the three boys and go to the city council to explain that our time as guests was over and that we had no roof over our heads. We set off like an army on the march, two three-week-old babies in a twin pram, a 2-year-old perched on top, and some bags stuck underneath it.

I arrived at the City Hall, a grey Victorian edifice, very distinguished and monumental in style, ornamented with large muscular ladies and gentlemen in flowing draperies. The clock in the tower overhead struck eleven. "The eleventh hour", I said to myself and helped Rueben up the steps. I did not have Tom alongside this time; he was working. But I would manage somehow. He told me that time before he was always with me, and I believed him.

I left the pram outside. A kind porter said he'd keep an eye on it. I got lost a few times in the warren of corridors before I found the right department. The housing officer was a bit astonished, but he could see I was very determined. Yes, he would do what he could. He made a phone call and then told me what to do. I would be given seventy-two hours accommodation at a hostel for homeless women with young children.

The place was on the edge of town, about four miles off. I set out pushing the pram and just trudged on, taking my time. I called in at Tom's mum's house, fed the babies, and then went up the hill to our new lodging.

The matron was expecting us and showed me a bed in a large dormitory in the attic. Cots were provided for the children. Seventy-two hours' accommodation. I didn't understand what this meant. It seemed reasonable, but I suspected it wasn't going to be long enough. I suddenly felt very weary. I'd always been with Tom, every evening since we set up house together he'd been there to share whatever I was doing, to talk about our day, to tackle the jobs. He'd help with anything. Do a bit of ironing, wash dishes, change a nappy. Sometimes he would read to me in a quiet, flexible voice. When I was pregnant he had me falling about with laughter with those funny, sad words of Gwyn Thomas about life in the Welsh mining valleys.

I sat alone in the empty dormitory feeding our twins. I would put a pillow under each elbow and suckle them, holding a small, sweet head in the palm of my hand, the babies' bodies lying comfortably along the pillows. Rueben sat on the floor or wandered about the strange room. He had a little car which he clutched vehemently – an object he felt sure of.

The matron came up and stood by, watching. I felt naked – I was. "Tomorrow we'll arrange your day. Everyone works in the morning on the housework. You'll do your share, but you'll be given time to bathe and feed your twins first. All the older children will be in the dayroom until lunchtime. One of the mothers is put in charge of them".

Later, in bed, I put my head on the pillow and wept. It was all so different, so organised. I felt imprisoned.

After breakfast a woman came and collected all the children to mind them while their mothers did the chores. Rueben was two and a half, and he had never been away from me. He began to cry. Someone picked him up and carried him, screaming desperately, into another part of the house. I went upstairs to feed the twins and after that to scrub the wooden floor of the attic.

I could hear Rueben's voice all the while. He sobbed incessantly and called out, "Rueben wants Rueben's mummy".

I wept too, and the tears mixed with the soapy water on the floor. The day dragged on. Rueben sat tearstained and bewildered, looking at me with reproach, with disbelief as we ate our lunch. I had deserted him and could not help him to understand. He clung to me, whimpering, when I took him with me to a field nearby to play. He had never whined like that – I felt like joining in.

We'd been told we could leave the house one night a week to visit our husbands. If we wished to see them before that we must meet them outside. No men were allowed in the hostel. Tom came that evening, when the boys were all asleep. We walked down the lane at the back of the house. His parent's house was full of his large family, his brother and three sisters and his parents; he was sleeping on the floor of his grandmother's room.

He'd managed to change his job to something nearby. This one was in a rubber factory; later he came from work with small burns all over his hands from handling hot moulds. He admitted to being clumsy. "Too bad I'm so ham-fisted".

The days passed. I discovered that the little children in the dayroom had no toys or equipment to help them through the morning. The more aggressive ones would pass the time squabbling, the mother in charge doing her best to keep the peace. Rueben sat day after day, never playing, crying bitterly for most of those three hours. One day he escaped and wandered off into the main building; he found his way to the room where we slept. I was there feeding the twins. He came upon me not anticipating anything, and a look of grief and amazement filled his face. He didn't say a word but climbed into his cot with his face turned away, sucking his thumb.

I felt that he wanted to forgive me for being with his brothers and not with him but could not reason it out. All he knew was that I had left him to cry so long, so long.

I told Tom about this and he comforted me. "Look, Jo", he said. "Things always change around my birthday. You've been in the hostel nearly four weeks, and they are bound to give us a house soon. Then we'll really make it right again. Jonah and Joseph will get their brother back".

Tom was tired. He had come straight from work in that evil-smelling factory, the stink of burnt rubber in his clothes, blisters on his hands. I took them and would have healed them if I could. It began to rain. We had been standing in the lane by the hostel, and there was nowhere to go. Some lorries had been parked for the night in a piece of waste ground across the way. We went over and Tom tried a couple of doors; one of them was unlocked. We climbed up the high step into the cabin and sat dry, watching the rain splashing the windscreen as the grey night came on. It was a shabby place; the seats had tears where the padding was oozing out, and there was an oily smell, some old rags on the floor. Someone had left empty beer cans behind. But it was good shelter and warm. I sat on Tom's lap with his old working coat on top of us both, and a great peace enveloped us, transforming, infusing us with its radiance. This was all the married life we could get, and we were having it abundantly. It got dark, and streetlights glowed through the misted glass. Very quiet except for the sound of drizzle making a gentle stir on the cabin roof. We must have slept a little.

I jerked up suddenly, my mother's intuition alert. "Better get back to the kids – it's been more than an hour".

Prelude

Arms all around: a big squeezing hug, and we tore apart. I ran quickly into the house.

Every month the welfare committee would meet on a Friday. All the mothers came up for review. The ones who were 'good' were allowed to stay, and the others were sent out to sleep rough, maybe. Their children were put into homes. Huge tensions would build up as the women waited for their turn. Tears and backbiting. Despairing silence; some would wet themselves out of fear.

The mothers in the hostel lined up to go before the committee. We went in one at a time. As I waited my turn, my mind raced through the possibilities, my faults before me. The time I had gone for a walk with the three boys, pushing the big pram to a recreation ground where Rueben could have a swing, I remembered when I was halfway there that I had left the wet nappies lying on the floor by my bed after changing the twins. I'd run all the way home in a panic, sweating, and dashed in to find them and put them away. I never dared to ask if anyone had noticed, but I knew that if someone had I would have that mark against me when it came to the chance of a house. I had been learning fast. I had to keep things tidy now. With three little ones, there was no time for anything else; no distractions like reading, which before had kept me from the housework. I realised that I was responsible for what happened to me, to our little family. I was going to work hard and get it right. Other women seemed to be orderly by nature; everything around them would be neat and clean. I wasn't like that. I had to train myself like a gardener training a rose to climb a wall. I was a housewife now, so I'd do just that. It would be as creative as making a picture. I was very clumsy, a beginner, and I was going to make a lot of mistakes, but they would not be such serious ones. I would really work at it.

One of the twins, Joseph, had become ill. A breastfed baby, they took him off to hospital and put him on a bottle. For ten days I was only permitted to see him through a glass panel. When he returned to me his tiny face was pale, and his eyes looked curiously enlarged. He had lost weight and cried often.

One morning as I was feeding them before breakfast, I suddenly felt a wave of nausea. I couldn't see properly – all dark at the corners of my view. I felt dizzy. When I brushed my hair it began to come out in handfuls; all day the dizziness and weakness persisted. I fought to keep my strength to suckle the boys, but I realised I was flagging. My body had been used all up to provide that milky flow, and there wasn't enough of me. The milk kept coming, but my metabolism couldn't keep pace. There was a debt somewhere, and it needed paying. So I put the babies on a bottle every other feed, and gradually I adjusted to a better balance.

A few days before Tom's birthday, just as he had predicted, we were allocated a welfare house. We could be in it before Christmas. It was five months since we had come into the hostel, and as we sat in our favourite lorry cabin, we planned and dreamed of home ahead and the good times we would have. Plant a garden and grow our own veggies, flowers too, make huge family cakes, bake bread, have folks to stay, a Christmas party, birthdays, pick blackberries for jam – and many more good things we would do together. We didn't analyze or think very far-off things. It was enough to have a 'now' to come to in our minds.

The house was on an estate to the north of the town, close to the hills and meadows. It was a new start. Tom had never once reproached me or blamed me in any way for being the cause of our separation. He did not feel that way. He shared all of it with me and did not have an impulse inside that makes a grumble. He did not compare or complain.

The house was so new that the paint was scarcely dry; the garden was a mud patch with builders' refuse scattered around. The row of twelve houses was raw, incomplete. One or two had curtains and looked warm. We had very little furniture: a bed, a couple of armchairs, a folding table. We went to junk shops and got second-hand bits and pieces. The day we moved in, just before Christmas, we lit a big fire in the empty living room and all slept in the room together, the babies in their pram and the three of us on the floor. We were home.

Life on a housing estate was not exactly bliss. Tom got a job in the steelworks, on shifts. He worked seven days as overtime was the rule, and we saw but little of him. Days would go by when he would never meet his little boys, leaving home before they woke and returning after they were asleep.

Time with him was precious, and we would go out in the country or work in the garden together. It began to flourish. We had good neighbours, and people gave us plants and roots. We sowed a lawn and got a good crop of vegetables.

Two years passed. Rueben was 4 and went to school. Tom went to and from work, patiently, bringing back his pay packet, which he always gave to me unopened. We'd sit down and sort it out, putting money in a jam jar for the rent and electricity. We didn't have much, but it was enough. I could manage, even save a little. There was always, root deep, a feeling of wholeness. Tom would come home from the night shift and very quietly come into bed. He'd put an arm around me and melt into sleep and warmth. I'd lie awake, waiting for the boys to call me for the potty, and listen to the waking birds as they sang in the dark. Tom, dozing off, would feel for my hand and turn the wedding ring on my finger round and round. I was his wife. He was reminding us of that.

When I married, an old uncle had written his wisdom to us. "You have been 'in love'", he said. "Now you are married; you will not be 'in love', you will love, plain, ordinary, daily love".

I used to pray sometimes, though I was not religious. I prayed, "Give us this day our daily bread," and I meant 'daily love', and not least the times in bed.

A lively, healthy family, a home and a little garden. Tom in work and good friends and family in abundance. It looked like a permanent thing. But there was a restlessness somewhere; it just didn't seem enough. A faint longing was there – but for what? Tom's long hours away from home, the tiredness that prevented the brief leisure time from fulfilling our needs, a great wish to learn more, to see more; all this was persistent in the background of our busy days. The life we had was like that of many others, and they seemed quite pleased to stay that way. We were not. We didn't talk about change or a move. But one day Tom came home with a newspaper page marked with an X. An advertisement announced a cottage to let – the Forestry Commission would rent it to a worker, job and home together. It was in the Wye Valley.

"Why not?" we asked and we applied for it. We went down to see it, riding in the little one-track railway, down through the trees and the woods of the river, past Llandogo and beyond. A tiny halt by the broad swift flow of the Wye, and we were at Whitebrook. Past a few houses hidden in the trees, a walk in the soft rain up a rough track under laden cider apple trees, and the cottage was there. Three floors tall, it was an old grist mill built of solid stone. The dwelling itself began at the top of sixteen stone steps built into the side of the house. The front door was above a stone porch which opened at ground level into a large space which had been the mill room. A huge grinding stone had once turned there, powered from the mill wheel in the stream outside. We went inside, the boys scrambling to the edge of the opening to watch the racing water.

We all felt elated. The little valley, full of young larch trees and the sound of rushing water was a place to live and grow things – us. The garden on the upper level, into which the house leaned like someone sitting in a high-backed chair, was a veritable Eden of promise. It had been the mill pond and was now silted up. The soil was very black and fine, on one side the mill stream, on the other a wall forming a terrace above. The wall was built against the hillside, and many sweet herbs grew in it, plus wild geraniums, wallflowers, and a stone crop.

We had no questions besides, "When can we come?" There was no gas or electricity, and the water supply was a pipe from the stream running through a tap into the house. The toilet was a wooden shack in the garden, there was no bathroom and we would need a zinc bathtub, which we could hang on the wall outside to store. It was 1956; the wages for a forest labourer were £7.13. The rent was 6s. 8d.

"Yes", we said.

We sat on the train going home and talked all at once. There was a tiny school in the village where the boys could go. We could grow our own vegetables in that amazing soil, and keep chickens. There was firewood in plenty from the forest. Perhaps we could get a second-hand Rayburn stove to replace the old open grate cooking stove in the big chimney place.

We packed our goods and chattels and dug out the best plants from the garden and stowed them in the old torn pram, and we hired a van cheap from a friend in the haulage business. Everything in and the two armchairs last, for the boys to sit on as we travelled. The three adults sat in the cab, and the kids jumped merrily at being left to themselves in the back.

I felt suddenly uncertain. I put my hand in Tom's as we sat together on the lorry seat. He squeezed it and just slowly nodded. I felt clear again. It was a fine day in late August, a hint of autumn in the sunshine, a little haze around the trees.

We turned off before Chepstow and went up the valley road. Then we left the main road behind and slowly wound our way along narrow country lanes until we reached the village.

Our lorry man took a look along the track to the cottage. "Can't take you up there", he said firmly. "Trees too low, and it's too narrow".

We started to take everything out and piled it all up on the side of the lane. The boys took a small chair each, and we all began to walk up this track to the mill, about half a mile. I pushed the old pram and arrived first. Meanwhile, a forest officer drove up and, taking in the situation, turned up half an hour later with a tractor and trailer.

We had a very busy afternoon getting to and from along the lane, up the sixteen steps and back again. The boys were small, but they did their share and rode on the tractor as well. Finally, as dusk came, we were done. We were country folk now and would work it out as best we could.

Tom lit the old stove and soon had it roaring. The oven heated up, and I took some apples, windfalls that the boys had found in the lane, and made a pie. We'd brought out the lamp and sat to eat in this mellow light, glad of the warmth, glad to be together.

Spring came and with it the sun. Our mill house and its garden had no shine during six weeks of the winter, because the valley was so deeply cut that the sun did not rise above the hillside, even at midday. The frosts enveloped the garden, and the washing on the line hung rigid, pants and shirts stiff as scarecrows. We began to garden again. The frost had broken up the clods, and a fine sweet tilth developed under our rakes and forks. We planted seeds and put up stakes for our beans. We had good hopes of a harvest but nature out-realised our wildest dreams. The Brussels sprouts spread out like umbrellas, a full yard across, the sprouts themselves as big as a man's fist. The lettuces were heavy-hearted, big as footballs, and the runner beans lived up to their name of yardstick, at least halfway. There were sugar peas, garlic and kohlrabi, calabrese, and an overflow of onions. The potatoes were the best we had ever tasted: golden wonder, small and waxy. We had herbs a-plenty too; mint, sage, thyme, and many others had been brought up in that old pram from the council house. The chickens began to lay tiny eggs at first, and the boys would love to hunt for them, laid mischievously in the undergrowth at the edge of the larch wood above the deep litter house. Later in the year one rogue chicken stocked away thirty-six eggs in a secluded nest, discovered accidentally when Jonas was climbing the wire fence around the young forest.

The days passed as flowingly as the wide Wye in the big valley below. Sometimes looking out over our little one we found it filled with mist, the trees sticking out of it here and there, a mysterious scene of isolation, as if we were transported to a mountaintop, the cottage standing above the clouds.

Tom's work as a forester took him far and wide across the hills and valleys. He cut and trimmed and gardened the young saplings, bringing the wood down from the forest rides, planting the spruce, fir, and larch seedlings in the spring. The three boys roamed free in the woods and fields, or all of us went on long walks, or gathered round another woodcutter's hearth for a mug of home-brewed cider and a slice of cider apple pie.

Saturday afternoons were sometimes an occasion for a journey to the market town to catch the little diesel train to Monmouth at the halt by the river. The one carriage was filled with valley folk and their families. A cheerful familiarity extended through the crowd of passengers, who exchanged pleasantries and jokes. The driver of the train saw Mrs Jones running down the hill, late as usual. He blew his whistle to encourage her, and waited for her to puff on to the platform before clanking on his way. The river slid by, silvery in the afternoon sun, and the curve of the bank unfolded the next vista of tree-robed hills. In town, we bought country necessities, seeds, or Wellington boots, or a new wick for the lamp, and crumpets to bring back in triumph to the kitchen fire.

That autumn was golden. A glistening harvest of enormous blackberries appeared in the lanes, apples in abundance. The plums were dropping off the trees. We dug the garden and planted up with winter kale and cabbage and ordered seeds for the spring. I bottled fruit, and we went to Monmouth market for a box of day-old chicks. A neighbour lent us a broody hen, and before long there was a crop of sturdy young fledglings pecking about on the upper terrace.

Tom would leave the house at six a.m. with an old kettle tied to his canvas shoulder bag. This was to make tea. The woodcutters would light a fire, boil water, and put the tea straight in it. The result was strong, a crudely flavoured, powerful refreshment. As the days got shorter, Tom would be home by four o'clock. During the long winter evenings we had time for talks, much reading, and radio play.

Bath nights were especially good. A huge pan of water was boiled to fill the big zinc tub. Boys in first, and a good back scrub into the bargain. We'd open up the fire door of the Rayburn and bask naked in front of the glowing logs to dry off. Rueben discovered his shadow, cast clear on the white wall. He danced to it, a young warrior shaking his imaginary spear, springing round in the lamplight, throwing his legs and arms in splendid gestures of victorious delight. Jonas and Joseph painted a boat on a roll of old wallpaper, six feet long, displayed joyfully along the length of the kitchen. The house was partitioned with tongue and grooved panels, fixed by a ship's carpenter who was employed to convert the mill into a dwelling. It sometimes felt like being on board a ship, with the water constantly gushing in the millrace at the side of the house.

Winter rains were heavy that year. The stream above the mill rose high, threatening the bank, lapping to within a few inches of our garden. Neighbours in a cottage close by warned that one year previously a tenant had been flooded out when the stream poured over the upper level and made its way through the garden, down the steps into the kitchen, and out again through the front door, where it splashed merrily down those sixteen steps to the yard and back into its own bed thirty feet away. We filled sacks with sandy soil from the upper terrace and lugged them down to the bank of the stream, calculated the spot most likely to give way, and sat up waiting the verdict. Our wall of sacks was sturdy and reinforced with stones. The water rose higher until a puddle arose on our side of the wall. Finally we gave up and went to bed. We had done what we could. We left the front and back doors wide open, with the comment that it might as well flow freely if it was going to flow. The kitchen next morning was draughty but dry. The stream stayed within its banks and never threatened us again.

It is a time of stillness, like the smoke spiralling gently out of our chimney pot, a lavender-blue transparency against the deep-green of larches beyond. We are not conscious of time passing. We are like a small boat wafting up and down as the waves swelled and dropped under us. We remain where we are as the undulating days pass.

The seasons were punctuated by visits from the outside world. A sister came, and then another, with young family to whoop and run in the hills and ripple into the Wye, wading the muddy edge to reach the faster flowing water midstream. At home in the evening we sat under the lamp and talked long, aware at a great distance of the turbulent doings of the weary planet, caring but uninvolved. It seemed enough to feed the hens in the morning and dig up a few more potatoes for lunch, wring out the heavy, wet sheets for the line, or bring half a tree down the hillside to chop for the fire. We were proud of our small valley, as if we had owned it for a thousand years. We rejoiced when town friends came and settled for a bit of peace.

A letter came one day from one such. Her husband had been killed when he came off his motorbike in March. It was a significant death. I burst into tears as I read her bitterly simple description of the event, and found myself writing to her in a way I had not done before. I felt myself an agent of this dead man's hand, to put into words the everlasting warmth of him, and thus to praise her and glorify her, who was his beloved. She was pregnant and later gave birth to a son.

One morning I got up at five and went up into the meadow above the mill. This field was full of wild daffodils, growing in huge clusters, spread like butter across the grass. The field adjoining was enclosed by ancient trees. Climbing the rough wall enclosing it, I was in a grey silence, the daffodils filling every space within the perimeter of trees, a luminous, delicate yellowness like moonlight at harvest time. I walked into them, picking a huge bunch of the tiny flowers, unable to avoid treading on some of them, they grew so close together. The sky was only just light, the sunrise far off yet. Some birds were beginning to sing, and then suddenly they burst out in a deafening chorus.

I went back to the house, collected a few things, and made my way to the railway to catch the work train. I took daffodils across England to Cambridgeshire and put them into my widowed friend's hand.

Her little son said, "I think it will be fine if I don't have to see a grown-up cry". He was seven.

I wrote to Rosa every week for many months. I had no choice. I felt sometimes that what I wrote had nothing to do with me, not me writing at all, but was a lot to do with him.

Two years filled up like water in a tidal pool. The second Christmas came; we exchanged messages with Lucy and Jock, my sister and her anthropologist husband. He told Tom to think more about using his mind as well as his hands. Our talks together had given him the impression of a lively mind which should be used to the full, not only in terms of some daily labour in the forest.

It was a seed planted. Tom began to talk about a further stage, a possibility of study, perhaps a place at Ruskin College for working men. Early in the summer he had a bad bout of lumbago. The doctor forbade him to work or bend his back. He got his sick certificate and took an enforced holiday for two weeks. He went upstairs to the sunniest room and started writing. Ruskin College required an essay on any subject chosen by the would-be student. He chose 'freedom'. He sent it away and quickly came the reply, to attend for an interview in Oxford. We got up early that morning, and he put on the dark-grey suit he'd bought when he tried to sell *Encyclopaedia Britannica*. He never wore a tie and always looked a little unkempt. His dark, curly hair wouldn't stay down and hung about his face. He would attempt to brush it flat again with his hand, a slightly clumsy gesture, a trifle self-deprecating. He looked very handsome and respectable. He felt himself on the brink of some huge change; he looked sombre, his eyes somewhat larger than usual.

He would be back next day, and I turned out the house while he was gone, polished the kitchen and washed the curtains.

He returned looking somewhat weary but elated. It had gone well, but another man had been offered the place. He had reservations about accepting it, so the first refusal would be Tom's. He'd have to wait and see. A week passed and then another.

One evening after supper he walked up the path to the edge of the forest and stood a long time looking out across the valley. I guessed he was ill at ease and wandered after him. The air was warm, soft with the smell of the first spring leaves and grasses. I came up beside him and he looked down at his feet. I put my arm around him and raised his head.

He looked back at me, and then a bewildered look, a mixture of frustration and uncertainty, filled his eyes. "I want to go so much, but it's all so difficult – you and the boys here, and there's no grant for a wife and kids. If I get a place, and I may not, how are you going to manage all those weeks on your own?"

His slight Welsh accent became a little stronger. "It's not easy, this waiting for an answer. I know they wanted me to have a place, but time is going on. I feel a bit wretched about it, almost wish I hadn't made the attempt. If I don't manage to go I'll always be wishing I had!"

It had grown nearly dark as we talked. He suddenly threw his arms around me and hugged me very close. We walked slowly back to the cottage, his arm still around my shoulder. A bird flapped out of the larch wood and flew with long, deep strokes of his wings, out across the sky which was a cloudless violet blue, luminous with one or two stars. The valley trees were clear and focused. Far down near the river a dog was barking.

The light was lit in Rueben's room, so we went up and sat on his bed. The twins heard us and tumbled in to join us. We all sat on the one bed and listened to a story. We were reading *The Hobbit*, a book lent us by the people who ran the guest house down the road. The story was about a journey made by little people and some dwarves, going off to find a treasure hoarded by an ancient dragon. Reading aloud was a great family ritual, to gather and sit down together, entranced into some wonder world or other. This was the first long book we had read to them; before it had been short picture-book stories. This was different, and a whole time and place were being unfolded. We felt ourselves being drawn into its realness, deeply concerned for the future of these folk, now our friends. It was our best entertainment. Tom and I would read in turns, and the words would flow out as we warmed to the adventure. Tom had a special, vivid skill in this, and the three boys would chorus a shrill protest when it was time to stop.

This particular evening, when we carried the lamp back to the warm kitchen, we sat with a mug of tea at the big table, just sipping, not talking.

"It will come out right" I said. "It surely will". Later we lay in bed, where we could see down the dark valley from our tiny open window. "Tom", I said, "you gave me not only bread but wine as well".

Loving each other was not so much a making as a being made. We were carried, borne out on a wide current into the middle of a river,

Prelude

entwined in its flow to arrive at the ocean itself and lose ourselves in its immensity, no time, no place, an unbounded fullness; burst back to the shore, laughing, shouting, exultant, and then lie silent until sleep quickly returned us to the ocean by another route. I sometimes wondered if that was what death was, another route to the same place.

As often, Tom got up first, not waking me, to tiptoe downstairs to brew himself a cup of tea. And then the long walk, sometimes an hour or more to the work site. Today I woke before he left, and at first light I went part of the way with him. When I came back, the boys were awake, and we were soon busy with breakfast and finding their socks. A letter came. The postman drove his red van up the narrow lane and parked in the yard. I ran down the steps to collect it. It was from Oxford. I didn't open it but put it on the shelf over the Rayburn.

Tom saw it as soon as he came through the door that evening. He opened it carefully, not rushing. "We would like to offer you a place … not necessarily lead to any academic qualification".

My eyes blurred over, because I knew he wanted it very much. I knew I would do absolutely anything to make sure he could go.

A time of plans and portents. Letters were written here and there; the local authority said he was too old for a grant. I decided to apply for a job, my first in seven years. Newport, the nearest large town, was twenty-five miles away. The little railway had just been closed, so our transport to town involved walking two and a half miles to the main road at Bigsweir Bridge over the Wye. Travelling to and fro by bus would be well-nigh impossible, involving too much time away from home and the boys. Somehow, money must be found, and I would buy a motor scooter, travel independently.

We took a friend's advice and applied to Tom's old regiment. We were interviewed by a retired soldier in Monmouth, a gentle, silver-haired old man with a courteous manner who questioned us carefully and long about our need for help. He seemed convinced and promised to recommend us. Sure enough, and very quickly, a cheque arrived for the price of a new Lambretta scooter, to be repaid, without interest, over a period of two years out of my teacher's salary. I had never driven anything with an engine before, not even a sewing machine, so at first I just sat on the back and leaned against Tom while he drove it home from the shop. It was pale grey, and I thought it was beautiful.

"Both of us", I pointed out. "Two minds but with a single thought".

He laughed. A bicycle made for two. It was hilarious, and I soon learned the ways of it, driving merrily up and down the narrow lanes of the wide valleys. We even piled the boys on it, illegally – one on the pillion seat, one in the carrier behind, and one standing on the platform between my knees – to reach the bus stop.

All through the summer the scooter was out and about; I'd feel like Brunhilda on her steed, my hair flying out behind from under my crash helmet. My sister lent me £10 to buy a complete outfit to wear in cold wet weather; a huge plastic coat with shoulder flaps, knee length 'flying boots', and big gauntlet mittens. I felt pleased with my gear, almost wishing for bad weather to try it out. I failed my first driving test, defeated by a roundabout, a one-way street, and not being able to drive at walking pace without wobbling.

Meanwhile, a job came my way. A secondary modern school in Newport urgently needed an art teacher, and I could start in September. It was arranged for the wife of the house next door, the only other cottage in our tiny valley, to come in and get the boys off to school and be there when they came back. She could do some housework while she was there as well.

The first two weeks I had Tom to come back to. He had left the forest job and was doing his first bit of reading for college, but he had the tea ready and the table laid. It was fifty miles a day to drive, but the road was beautiful and the ever-changing weather, the fruit trees mellowing in the late summer sunshine, made the time pass. I enjoyed it.

School was less charming. I quickly discovered that it was an unhappy place; a bitter atmosphere prevailed; the teachers and pupils embattled, a cane in every teacher's desk. I was given a lot of kindly help and had much to give back, but the style of the place was set. I could not go against it single-handedly and my own instinct for a natural growth in creativity. Using encouragement and enthusiasm was overwhelmed by the harshness of the conflict which seemed to be rooted deep in the nervous system of the school. A great stress was there, working its way out in the turbulent and frustrated youngsters, fanned by angry teachers. I soldiered on through this and said little when I got home, glad to forget.

The day came for Tom's departure. He would be gone for twelve weeks. Back for Christmas. He dug the garden and planted some winter cabbage. There were still plenty of vegetables growing and coming up, and apples and plums were in abundance; the hens were thriving.

We all went down to the bus together. He took his case on the scooter and then ferried everyone in relays. The weather was soft, rain tipped, with scurrying low clouds just above the valley trees. We grabbed each other, the man, the woman, and the three boys all in a huddle. Then onto the bus and we stood waving on the quiet roadside as it disappeared between the trees.

I put all three boys on the scooter and drove back at ten miles an hour. I felt as if I'd left something behind, but I wasn't afraid or anxious. We were all going to be busy, doing what was proper to do. Everyone in the hamlet had heard about our doings and I was given a lot of goodwill and kindness in the thoughts and comments of the people I met. The tiny shop/post office was a pleasant place for a gossip. We dropped in on the way home and the boys chose some sweets.

"Well, Mrs, you're on your own now – grass widow for a bit. But you'll be OK; if you need anything you let us know". Thus the postmaster's wife, a tiny, round woman, rather akin to the jars which stood in their round, well-ordered rows filled with coloured boiled sweets and bright wrapped toffees. The shop had a curious mixed smell of bacon and cheese, cough sweets and fresh bread, and the musky odour from sacks of chicken feed in the corner. I felt grateful for the kindness and knew that there would be more.

We mustered ourselves and marched up the lane under the apple trees, gathering a few windfalls as we went. Cider apples are tiny and not sweet, but they are strong flavoured and we'd stew them up for their juice, drink it hot, flavoured with ginger and cinnamon.

My daily journeys to school came and went in a succession of blowing leaves and autumn winds. The early morning would be adrift with the valley mist lying over the river. Tintern Abbey lost in a fold of gold light when the sun shined on its shroud of vapour, the trees copper and brass and rusty iron, colours of metal, soundless in the October sun.

I vehemently fought for peace at school, but I didn't win. The children were beaten with canes. This was routine in the 50's, in village schools, (and in the schools for the wealthy like Eton and Harrow). Nevertheless beautiful pictures began to emerge from the chaos as the children responded to the joy of painting them – I made that lively to them. But I was losing control. My friendly art room was a temptation to many of the pupils who had lost patience with life, parents, teachers, and all. A war was on. I was an easy option, a battlefield with no defence. One day I borrowed a cane, and for the first time I hit out at my pupils. I was aghast at the enormity of it. I trembled.

A few days later the first frost came. Early in the morning the innocent road wound under the trees, lovely and self-possessed. I came down a hill and saw a large puddle lying across the way. I accelerated a little to bring the scooter through it, and as the front wheel came out of the wetness, there was a patch of black ice, and a violent movement pitched the front forks aside. I was on the ground, my head reeling with pain where I had hit it through my crash helmet. I was not knocked out but very shaken. The place was deserted, miles from anywhere, so I got on the scooter, which was still running, and went on my way. Some instinct told me to go to school and carry out my duties rather than go back to the house where the boys would be getting ready for school.

My head ached heavily, and when I took my crash helmet off, I found a huge swelling over my left brow. My first class came in, and I explained briefly what had happened. They listened and then got on with what I asked them to do.

After an hour I felt dizzy and was soon violently sick, a reaction I might have expected and should have been prepared for. I felt in some way that the violence in this school and my share in it had reaped a harvest in my head. I had sown a dragon's tooth and reaped it. Obviously there was no more teaching that day. The school secretary, a kindly, middle-aged woman, made no fuss and took me home. I had time to get my bearings before the boys came in for their tea. It was Friday afternoon, and the weekend ahead to ease my head – and my heart.

Tom wrote, and I to him, about once a week. He was delighted, even amazed by the fulfilment of his needs, the very fact of having time to read books, to have them available, the discussions and exchange of

Prelude

ideas. This was an extraordinary change in his way of life where manual labour had filled his working day. Ruskin College was a collection of people from all kinds of working backgrounds and ages, many of whom had left school, as Tom had, when they were 14. They were all hungry and thirsty for the expansion of their minds and had huge appetites for growth.

I said nothing of my doings on the high road this time but told him what the boys had been up to. The next week all was well again and I could tell him so. A new side mirror on our scooter and a touch of paint over a scratch, and my transport recovered too, though not so new looking now.

I quickly learned to account for the weather hazards on my route and to use my feet as stabilisers – not as easy as it would have been on a regular motorbike. But I had the windshield to shelter me from bitter winds, and that was a compensation. I stopped using the cane, though I kept it in my desk.

Tom arrived and we met him triumphantly at the bus stop by the river, put him on the scooter for the first relay up the valley, and then finally we were all in the warm lamp-lit kitchen, aglow with our togetherness, hugging, laughing, talking all at once. Steaming mugs of tea and a huge homecoming cake – Aunty Alice cake we called it, after Tom's mum, who had shown me a traditional recipe of her family. Later we sat in front of a log fire, all five of us squeezed together on the sofa, and Tom read as never before; his range of expression to act a part, to give us the feeling of the scene, was deepened and more vivid. I sat and stared at him, couldn't take my eyes away. I was in love. I was overwhelmed with the thought, "This most wonderful man is my husband – what an incredible thing to have happened to me".

In my head I sang the 'Magnificat', the song of Mary, and my heart exulted. The boys looked radiant. We took a long time with them, sat on their beds gossiping and joking, and then, for the first time in so many weeks, my husband and I were alone together. We sat by the fire wrapped in the warmth of it and each other. Then to our bed to lie as one body and mind.

"Happy Christmas", said Tom.

It wasn't yet, but it was his birthday. I still had a few days left at school. It was a festival to come home each day, very cold from the hour on the scooter, to find the house bursting with light and lively talk, food ready, a total welcome.

Term over, we went out to find a Christmas tree. So many thousands to choose from! We brought back the biggest the house would hold, and on Christmas Eve, as was our habit, adorned it and set on it the little live candles in their tiny holders. These would be lit every day from Christmas to New Year's, just for a few silent minutes – the whole room hushed to the brilliance and warmth as the infant points of fire sparkled in the eyes of the five who watched and breathed in the aroma of pine awakened by the warmth of fifty live candles.

We had no visitors this year, exchanged greetings with neighbours in the nearby cottages, but saw little of anyone except our small family gathering. A few days of bliss. Walks in the woods, the frost crunching in the twigs and dead leaves, a great sawing up of logs with the old bow saw, one end each until our hands were blistered. Long talks in the evening as we planned ahead, and then Tom would develop some thought, how he had responded to some reading, which was mostly to do with social things, the balance in society, freedom, security, change, and such. An order based on compassion and justice.

He had done well this first term. It was clear he would be able to stay and do another whole year, making two in all. He began to understand that my job and journey were hazardous for me and think his long absences were adding to that. He wondered if I should move to another job, perhaps live closer to my work. I was not afraid of going on as we were but began to think of possibilities. I'd hear that in Cambridgeshire there were places called village colleges, where the rural communities could enjoy further education facilities which were combined with the local secondary school. They were specially built for the purpose, and the staff and their families were housed around the campus.

I had friends in Cambridge from teaching days before I had married Tom, and I resolved to go there and see what I could find out. As it turned out, to our great good fortune, a job was advertised in one such, to start just before Easter.

I set off for Cambridge with a folio of children's work and a lot of determination. I came back with a job for the following September, complete with a new home. The college had just been built. I could even choose the equipment for the art room, which also contained a new kiln and pottery. It was almost too good to be true. Work would be a hundred yards from the house, and there would be scope for all kinds of creative adventures for the boys and me. I could do evening classes with the college adults too, and it was certainly no further from Oxford than the Wye Valley.

I was beginning to feel a strong sense that the pattern of our life was unfolding ever more promisingly. I had one more term to do at my present school. Summer was benevolent; I took my classes out into the meadows, and somehow the atmosphere was sweeter, not least with the friendships that had developed with fellow teachers over the year. One day was given over to some special films ordered by the art department. There was one about William Blake, illustrated with his poems and drawings. I was enraptured. I felt vast, awesome feelings welling up from this view of the universe, of God.

"I will give you a golden string – only wind it into a ball – it will lead you to heaven's gate set in Jerusalem's wall".

"One law for the ox and the lion is oppression".

"Thou art a man; God is no more".

I suddenly felt that God was real. I'd had emotions like this from time to time, but this was more present, more intense than before. I longed to express myself, to respond. I wrote to Tom and told him how I felt, that maybe I should become a Catholic, which seemed the most enlivened form of Christianity I'd come across. (I was aware of a paradox because William Blake had no room for that form of religion.)

Tom was clear in his mind. He did not want this either! He felt it would separate us. He had only one view of religion – he believed in questions, in doubt. He felt that questions had an absolute quality; answers would be merely relative, changing and varying with time and circumstances.

I set aside my impulse but went to Mass sometimes, moved by something outside reason or common sense. And I said prayers too, as if seeking out a hidden essence of something nearer the centre of things, the order and compassion and wholeness we talked about. Tom and I found that centre wordless, whole and wholesome, like the thread of Blake's string in the love we made and gave. I knew it here and now, this time and place: guessed that other times and places represented the same thing and would do so for ever and ever, after and before. I felt than, but could not give it words, that we were part of something in the same way that water is the ocean. We were small scattered drops in that immensity, but were the whole of it as well.

The three boys were active and strong and immensely enjoyed their life together. Rueben was a leader, but not a bossy one. Jonas and Joseph were his loyal supporters in numerous adventures. They had the run of the valleys and woods. So far, school had almost been a game as well. The tiny school in the village had two classes. The twins shared one of them with another pupil, a little girl who was often absent. They enjoyed the benefits of learning the three Rs from a gentle old teacher who had lived in the place all her life and was as near to an old-dame schoolteacher as could be imagined.

Rueben was in a class of twelve. He learned to read and write and to enjoy painting pictures, but not much else.

The time for the move to Cambridgeshire was drawing near, and the boys remembered the big move to Cardiff and were eager for the next scene of the play. We shared all our plans with them, and the summer holidays went fast. The valley seemed all the more precious to us now that we were to leave it. We went for even longer walks than usual. The late summer lay like deep green velvet on the trees and the smell of larch logs burning was a meditative offering to the quiet sky – one time we saw a rainbow from the hilltop at Pen y Fan's green; it spanned the Wye like a bridge, and the zenith of its bow was seen in its prism of radiance, the dark, tree-bordered parabolic curve of the far side of the valley hanging far above it. Everyone held their breath as if the faintest whisper would blow it all away. Blackberries were just swelling, hanging all along the steep pathways through the forest, and we'd arrive home at the mill with purple fingers and tongues and a good pie-full in the bag.

Tom had taken a holiday job in Monmouth unloading a huge consignment of raw brown sugar at a warehouse. The rough crystals had made his shoulders raw, and he had many wasp stings from the attendant hoards that hovered over the labourers as they lifted the heavy bags with both hands and swung them over their backs. Once loaded, it was hard to fend off the vehement little stingers. He earned enough

Prelude

to pay for our move and took a few days off before term began to help pack up the house.

We had been married nearly eight years. The current of our activity felt strong, and we were swept along by it, not hesitating, borne up. We never questioned that deep impulse but flowed with it, irresistibly trusting it and each other for whatever lay ahead, no ultimate goal in view. We just did whatever was next to be done.

Melrath Village College was new. When we arrived, the men were there laying turf and cleaning up the builders' refuse. There was a smell of new wood and wax polish and the sweetish odour of new fabrics and carpets. The little house was trim and bare, the stairs echoing as we went up and down carrying boxes and blankets, toys and books. The Wye Valley was lost to the mind amidst the hubbub of the boys' questions, wanting to learn everything all at once. The Cambridgeshire water meadows and the wide fenland sky were washing the Wye out of our heads for the time being, pollard willows trailing in the riverbed, the wild watercress and the plush-headed bulrushes brown as a dog's nose. We had to tear ourselves away from these allurements to attend to our respective academic necessities.

The boys were off to the village school, much bigger and more formal than before. Tom returned to Ruskin, and I would face my new pupils and the teachers in a new building. Some of the teachers were my close neighbours and living a few yards from the college. It was all unfamiliar and yet the same – the first day of term with rows and rows of freshly washed faces in new uniforms, the clatter of tea cups in the staff room, and the art room smell of paint and clay. Our evening meal was a babble of busy talk about our experiences. We were still all together, the day for Tom's departure for Oxford drawing very close. When it came, we all went down to the station to wave him off and wish him joy. We hugged him and clustered around him, all arms round and heads together, loving him, sending him off. He would be back for half term, but it seemed a long way off.

We climbed up the little footbridge over the track and watched the carriages as they dribbled away down the lines. We walked home across the fields a bit silent but not discontented. There was work to be done. It was a busy time; the college work was demanding, and I gave it all I had.

The boys and I had good times together. The other teachers were always ready to help when a man's skill was needed in the house or garden. When I did the adult classes in the evening, I could see the boys' bedroom windows from my studio. They would flash the light on and off if they were in urgent need of assistance! Sometimes they would indulge in what was known as 'college prowl'. Eight-year-old Reuben and the twins, now 6, would creep into the dark campus and do the rounds of all the buildings, peeping into the lighted windows to watch the proceedings within, all unseen, and delighting in their invisibility, making ribald comments about mannerisms of teachers and students.

One evening Jonas was using his bed as a trampoline, and he tore his way through the spring framework. Our next-door neighbour rescued him by weaving a network with a piece of clothesline, which he proudly revealed next morning

The arts and crafts department began to flourish. The country children had plenty of imagination and responded with me to a wide range of creativity in ever increasing liveliness. Their art began to flow out from the studio and soon the school was embellished with vivid expressions of all kinds from the different age groups. We had a good time together; even the so-called dull ones could produce beautiful things. The local art adviser turned out to be a good friend and she encouraged me, stimulated my teaching, and gave me ideas about techniques and media.

The holidays arrived, and once more the reunion of the family with their man of the house produced such an atmosphere of joy that Christmas took on a sparkle that illuminated everything. It would be hard to imagine a greater happiness. Tom had decided to apply for a mature students' scholarship so he could go to a university when he finished at Ruskin. He spent some time writing an essay for this, and as before, it was on the subject of freedom. Later he would have to justify this essay before an exacting committee of judges.

My art advisor friend invited us to a meal, and once again a direction was found which we had not dared to hope for. A fellow guest was the tutor of a Cambridge college. He talked all evening with Tom, and when he had heard our story, he promptly invited Tom to apply for a place at

Cambridge. Sure enough, Tom got his scholarship, and the place at St. John's College as well. We were rather dazed with the way everything had fitted together – it was much better than we could have guessed at the beginning of all this.

The weeks flew by, spring came, and the summer term Arrived. One weekend in June the headmistress who was my neighbour came in to look after the boys, and I drove across the countryside on my scooter to Oxford to meet Tom. He entertained me in his little room-cum-study; the house was in a side street, a tiny cottage with rioting red roses in the garden. For the first time since the twins were born, I had the feeling that I would like another baby. But that could not be yet – our home depended on my job. I must be the breadwinner for a few years more.

I felt like a newly wedded bride in Tom's arms. The cottage was a honeymoon house; the red roses came in through the window, mind and hearts as entwined as they. He showed me everything, took me out to dine at the Oxford Union, and lovingly introduced me to his friends. His warmth was everywhere, and it overwhelmed everyone. He was like the sun at midday.

I went back with a gleam in my eye, glowing with the knowledge that very soon he was going to be at home for the lovely, lazy weeks of the summer vacation, and thereafter would be home every weekend. The vigil of those twelve-week terms away was almost over.

Cambridge beckoned. A lodging was found with an art teacher friend of ours. Like Tom she had started out later than most and became a student when she was bringing up her daughter single-handedly. Now she had a job in a country school, like me, and her home in Cambridge was an ideal spot for him to live and study. Tom would have the scooter and go to and fro five nights in town and two with us in the country.

Tom decided to read *Moral Sciences*, the Cambridge term for philosophy. He wrote his essays lying on our double bed, arms behind his head. He'd stay there, quite unmoving, for an hour or more, and then start writing vigorously. He worked, not always easily, but because he wanted to.

"It's unbelievable, Jo. All my life I've loved to read, and now they give me money to read the books I like!"

It was a time of steady, natural growth, like the garden when the seeds have sprouted. Time was needed and some maturing. We cherished each other and the boys. All together ... we always went together. If one went slower, the others waited. I read a lot too, and always we read to the boys.

Rueben began to read *The Lord of the Rings*. After a few chapters his courage failed. He was wise. "Mum", he declared, "I can't manage this yet; it's too scary. I think I'll try it when I'm 12".

What with the job and everything to do at home, the everyday pleasures, a pattern of life in which there were no dull moments or fears for the future created a sense of permanence, a settledness. But we knew we would be moving on. We always had – it seemed this was our way; to be at home somewhere and then to be like nomads and find another field. Sometimes I felt weary and hoped to be a housewife again, longed to suckle a child once more, do my housework, dig a garden, make bread, just be at home and be a helpmate for my man. The terms came and went and two years as well.

There had been death in our family during this time, Tom's mother, and also mine.

I was with my mother when she died. She went, sleeping, after nine years in bed following a stroke. She had lost her speech and could only say "no" (perhaps the first word she had learned). She had been able to use her only word to express any meaning, and often it was "yes". She had been a woman of lively words and great intelligence.

I held her hand as she died, watched the colour go from her quiet face, awed by the fact of her spirit leaving the body. An immense stillness infused the room, and when she had gone I stood a while, not moving at all, as if under a spell, not a thought in the mind, but a vast space like a cloudless sky at nightfall. An hour later I sat with my sister in a nearby cafe, not speaking much but feeling close and deeply related in this new experience. There came a moment, a clear instant of time when we both felt the same impulse. I caught it in her face and she in mine.

We both knew, innocently and spontaneously, that we were not alone. We were enveloped in a tranquil radiance of feeling and reassurance. Our mother was at home.

Not long after it was another's turn. A niece, beautiful and talented, a medical student, had lung cancer. She had already lost a leg, for the disease was rampaging through her system. She had become accustomed to this role of dying and had made friends with it. She lived, not fighting, but made every breath of hers a flight of joy. It was a wonder to her to remain alive at all. Our sons would romp with her, exchanging ribaldries with her about her artificial leg, and she would ride on the back of my scooter with it stuck out at a rakish angle. All too soon the fragile body faded, and she lost bulk like a withering flower. Finally she lost consciousness, lying in a cubicle in a London hospital. I drove down through the night and saw her lying there like the sleeping beauty. She had taken her anatomy books with her when she went into the ward; perhaps her sleeping mind was dreaming of medical school and all those realms of knowledge that her body represented.

She died that night – it was first of November, All Saints' Day. The boys missed her when they lit their bonfire on the fifth. She had promised to be there. I remember thinking that if ever I had a daughter, I would name her Esther after this 22-year-old who must surely have pleased the King immensely to have been granted an audience so soon. I felt she would make a splendid guardian angel.

Examinations were due, the final test for Tom. He sweated through them in a heat wave and declared himself satisfied with his second class honours degree. No urge for further study but a strong wish to earn his living and be our man at home again after these four years of student life.

He had been applying for jobs, and most of the ones he fancied were for people of his age group (he was 40) but with a mass of experience he did not have. One advertisement caught his eye – the words seemed almost poetic – the Vale of Catmose Village College wanted a tutor for further education. He knew the job well as our neighbour, our own Village College had that post, and he had observed its ways firsthand. He wrote off, tongue in cheek, telling them what it was all about, laying down an unconventional adventurous program of possibilities for work in a rural community. He was called for an interview, and boldly spoke his mind as he did not anticipate anything, and was promptly offered the job.

Time Out of Mind

Rutland was the smallest county in England. A soft, undulating landscape with miniscule hills and valleys, tranquil small rivers, and the mild ochre and muted strong purple of the Cotswold ironstone wherever a church thrust its spire or tower out of the clustered green of the village trees. We managed to rent a farmhouse in a tiny village not far from Oakham. It was very spacious and had an acre of ground. The farm itself was all around us; cow sheds, pigsties, chicken houses, haystacks, and all. We would wake at dawn to the sound of a multitude of tiny hoof beats passing in the road outside as a flock of sheep made its way into a nearby field, their guardian dogs barking discretely to the high-pitched whistles of their masters.

The village church was across the road. On Thursday evenings the bell ringers would practice their changes – a grand procession of vibrations would fill every corner of the house making conversation impossible. We would read, or better still, dig the garden to the rhythm of these marching bells. Looking up from the garden behind the house, the church tower rose high and delicately crenulated against the sky, a bright gold weathercock strutting atop the conical roof.

We all felt liberated. Tom set out to the new job. I stayed home to redecorate the house, to make bread, to start up the gardening where we could grow food enough and to spare. Weekends were resplendently busy, with much to plan and make. We had acquired an ancient car, an old blue Lanchester; very queen-like it was, with huge wheels and a long bonnet, running boards, real oak fittings inside, leather seats somewhat worn and torn, but grand comfort. The boys had innumerable delights; the fields and lanes, a pond or two, bikes, and an old tent. We quickly gathered to ourselves a cat and a dog.

I was absorbed and busy with the newness of homemaking, and the first days passed in a hurry. So intent was I in this that I scarcely noticed a shadow on Tom's face. He seemed puzzled by something but did not speak of it. Several times I was aware that he was more silent than usual, not so much that he chose to be but that it seemed to be forced on him. I wondered, and then got busy again.

The next few days were taken up with painting walls, filling holes in the plaster, and stripping wallpaper. I made a list of colours we would need for our dining room and sitting room, and we drove into town to get them. Something was amiss; I could tell that. Tom was angry. I had never known this before. We got the paint, and I somehow survived until the boys had gone off into the village after our midday meal.

I found Tom in the garden digging. I asked him straight out, "What did I do – is it me?"

And he answered me equally direct and clear: "Yes it is. You have entirely forgotten that this is our home, we are here together. But you haven't ever asked my opinion or planned any of it with me. You have left me out as if I were just another item in your list of paints. I may as well not be here for the amount of value you give to my being part of the household again after all this time. It's no good".

He did not offer any consolation for my dumbstruck face but turned back to his digging. I fled into the house and up to the bedroom, buried my head in the pillow, and howled fiercely for a while. He did not come. I felt deeply ashamed. I knew at once how it was. I had been alone at home for these four years. Tom had been an honoured guest in his own home when he came there in the holidays. But I'd had the responsibility. Now that the time to share again had come, I had let him down. I had not shared. I could not keep back the tears, the ache of it was so sharp. I didn't know how to begin to make amends for such a vast blunder in understanding – it seemed basic, irremediable.

I got supper, keeping my face away, talking with my back to the boys; hoping they wouldn't see my puffy eyes. I pleaded a headache and went to the bedroom again, without eating at the table. It got dark. I lay on my back, the tears still falling, and I knew nothing would be right until he came and told me I could be his wife again. For those few hours I felt I had been severed from him, utterly. It was a black hell. I wanted only one thing: to love him and share everything with him. I couldn't see how it would come out or that he would ever respect me again.

It seemed hours, and then I heard the door open. Tom appeared with a tray. On it was tea, an egg, and some toast. "Come on, Jo. You should eat something".

I sat up, unable to answer, still so full of shame. I drank some tea. Then, slowly, some words came. "I will never, never do that again – I didn't understand, I just didn't notice. I will get it right now, I know I will".

He sat, not speaking, and waited for me to eat. When I finished, he took the tray. Then he turned out the light and got into bed beside me. I was still in my clothes. He gently helped me to take them off, and we just lay very still for a time.

Then he turned, pulled my head over to his, and put his arm around me, closing his hand over mine. He felt my ring, his ring, and began to turn it on my finger, pushing it a bit further on. I sighed, a deep fluttering as when the crying has stopped and only the altered breath betrays it.

"It is all right", he said. "It will be better now".

We slept, and the morning was bright. We never spoke of this after but went on with the jobs. The sitting room was finished and filled with flowers – we sat down in it that first time and there was no shame or pain – only peace, and the bells chiming, stepping in their grand sequences in the church tower.

That Christmas we ordered a turkey. They were living in a stone outbuilding a few yards away. Christmas Eve came, and the expected bird had not yet appeared. I had a well-trussed, trim parcel in my mind's eye.

What came to our back door was an enormous flapping creature held out at arm's length by the farmer's daughter. "It's dead all right", she said.

I agreed, quite unbelieving – I grudgingly took the bird from her; the huge white wings convulsively brushing my arm as they opened and closed, chopping the air. I held it away and walked carefully into the large, brick-floored kitchen.

Tom and the three boys were roasting chestnuts by the open grate. "You look like the Ancient Mariner", said Rueben, who had done it at school last term.

It was a fine crisp day, and we hauled it outside again and plucked for what seemed a long time. The garden looked like a Christmas snowfall, feather flakes everywhere. We feasted well the next day, and the house glowed with candlelight. There was warmth in the hearth as the logs sparked and glowed and the hearts of every one of us were glowing too. Tom was a man who could not help spreading a pattern of goodwill, Christmas-like wherever he was. It oozed out of him naturally, like the warmth from the burning logs.

Prelude

This winter was a hard one. Snow came, and then more. Deep hoar frosts turned the lanes into magical ice tunnels. In the dark evenings we read aloud to the boys. We started the long journey through *The Lord of the Rings* and read ourselves hoarse with the utterances of Gandalf and his fellow travellers. The Lanchester got stuck in a snowdrift, and the big end broke. At long last the thaw came, and with the first signs of spring I discovered that I was pregnant. It had been a long time. The twins were now nearly 10, and I was nearly 40, but it felt the most appropriate thing. We all wanted this baby, and we all wanted a girl.

The nine months went fast. During the summer holidays we borrowed a trailer for the little van we had got second-hand to replace the Lanchester and went camping in Wales. It rained most of the time, and we walked on misty beaches, explored rivers and waterfalls, and eventually reached the foot of Cader Idris, the loftiest mountain in central Wales. I sat in a field with my load of baby and watched my four menfolk wending their way up the track to the top. The baby jumped around my belly, and I lay back in the sun and was content.

She was born in November. I had her in the little cottage hospital. I refused all anaesthetics this time as I wanted to participate in full alertness. She arrived with a problem! The umbilical cord was wrapped around her tiny neck many times, and she could not breathe. It took a long time to free her, and she was not yet breathing. A tiny whiff of brandy was given to her, and the gasp that broke through with the reflex to the powerful vapour was her first breath.

I was older than most of the other mothers, so I was put to share a room with a young one who had just had her first. She was an innocent country girl who had given birth without ever having known how things worked within her own body. She did not know how a baby was born until it actually happened. She was so frightened of this unprecedented experience that she was out of her mind for a while. It was thought I would be good company for her and help to reassure her.

I had never been close companion to someone who was 'mad' before, and at first I felt a little nervous. Soon I saw that she was just like everyone else, only that because she had not noticed some things she had become confused. I'd had the same experience – not noticing – when I had lost touch with Tom that time. Because of this I was aware of my neighbour, and she began to respond to that. In a few days she was talking and laughing quite naturally again.

Tom came to fetch us home. He tenderly, most carefully, carried his new daughter in his arms. We called her Esther, because she had found favour with the King. In the house we waited for the boys to return home from school. One by one they came into the warm kitchen and peered into the carry-cot, which was set on the hearth rug.

Jonas sat with his back to the fireplace. Rueben and Joseph stood by.

"Well", Tom said, "Who's going to hold their sister?"

There was a pause, and suddenly Jonas held out his arms. So he was the first. It was a blissful time. We were all enthralled by this new life. She was very responsive and soon laughed like a chime of tiny bells. We had been a family who loved and learned together, but never more than now, with this blessing of infancy in the midst of us. We rejoiced, and regained something. It was as if we were regenerated by our newest member. She gave us a vista of liveliness and growth. For Tom and me it was a refreshment of our being together, our love flowed and overflowed. We were fulfilled.

When she was 9 months old we left our rural arcadia and went to live in Southsea on the South coast, the residential part of Portsmouth, home to the British Navy. It was a big change to live in the middle of a busy town. Tom's new job was in an art college, where he could teach philosophy and encourage the art students in complimentary areas of creativity and knowledge. He was delighted with this and felt he had found a good place for his gifts as a teacher. We borrowed money from a friend and put down a deposit on an old-ish house, a fine Victorian three-storey one with room to spare for our growing family.

Life seemed to have an air of permanency and completeness about it. We bought an old Aga cooker, had the home rewired, and redecorated it together. The sitting room, especially, was very beautiful. Tom sanded the floor and polished it. We planned it all together, and the room represented that united awareness, and our sharing that had nearly failed to attain once before. We had no fears for the future. There was a life to live, much to learn, many new and cherished friends. Other people had problems and came to us for reassurance and support. We gave it, grateful for our own at-one-ment. The texture of life seemed ever deeper, wider, strand by strand of a beautiful connected pattern appearing and holding together in a bright design.

A time when it would not be this way could not be imagined or conceived.

Esther was growing more beautiful each day. She had the serenity and confidence that is the privilege of the youngest child. Her three brothers enjoyed themselves hugely with her, and also with each other. They acquired a canoe, and some masks and flippers, and took to the sea like dolphins. What would happen to us next? We had been wanderers, never staying very long anywhere. I suspected we would not evade this process; it seemed built-in.

Sure enough, Tom saw an advertisement for a job in his old college, Ruskin, in Oxford. He applied for it. It was after his own heart. He wanted to serve these people, to help the developing minds of the late developers, the non-starters who had started after all.

He was short-listed, and the interview was fixed. The weekend before, we went to Cambridge and stayed in a friend's home. Tom collected his MA degree from the Senate House, and we returned home in a hopeful frame of mind.

Then it all changed. But not as we had expected. It turned out quite different.

Fugue

We called our local bin the herb garden. Neil's idea. I met Neil in the outpatient area, and he announced this like the angel Gabriel. Neil is a gentle man, tall like a tree, an oak most like, looks like a lad, though he's older than 30 years old, and I think he's a child prodigy bottled up in a man's frame.

Sitting down with his huge shoulders hanging over the back of one of my old wooden chairs, his long big hands rather forlorn between his knees, he would stay, listening mostly, and then quite suddenly stand up and leave, but always leaving a gem of truth behind. Like the herb garden. This was a way of telling other folk that people from there were valid, real. Herbs in the garden are often not noticed; outside they appear un-pretty, rough-leafed, few charming flowers, growing low maybe, not raising their heads. But a little of that flavour in the right proportion makes an everyday dish memorable.

It was about this time that I began to write poems, and it's because of the poems that I'm writing this. Not many people read poems, and I didn't write them in the first place because I thought anyone would read them. I wrote them because I was in confusion, my mind swinging and soaring, unstable; I couldn't talk because no one could hear me; the poems were a way of telling, at least the paper and my own eyes as I wrote, more of what I was about. And I wanted to know what I was about – being mad means you don't, and when things happen in the mind, thoughts coming that you never dreamed to think, you become amazed and afraid because you are sure you can never understand how it works.

The whole process of being mad began at the ending of another process, or stem. But this one is all about that one too, growing out of it. And so it will be about Tom. Where he ended, all this begins.

Fugue

I have to stop here, actually, for a moment. A space of silence comes. It's because I can't move my pen. When Tom is in my mind that can happen; everything focuses into one place and is quite still. A broad man, middling tall, and a bit heavily built; you could see the Welsh origins there. He'd been a miner once, and a host of other things too; had workman's hands but gentle, grey-blue eyes, his pupils very full and black in the centre. Mr Valiant-for-Truth I'd nicknamed him in my mind, though never said it. His look totally dissolved you of stress, and his strength of kindness could scatter anxiety like sun on a May mist. He never wore a tie if he could help it and regarded himself a working man, a common man, which he was. His uncommon thing was that he was ordinary and wise as well.

Anyway, his heart stopped, late one evening, on Waterloo station. When they took him from the ambulance at St Thomas's Hospital he was dead, and a phone call was made to the police station in Southsea, next door to our home. I'd gone to bed, and when the front doorbell rang I got up and answered, thinking Tom had left his key behind.

A young policeman came in instead, and we both stood in the passage. He had the torn-off page of a notebook in his hand, and he read from it briefly. I could not think of anything to say. A space of silence came.

Then, slowly: "I don't understand what you've told me. I don't understand it".

I asked him to come into the kitchen, and I made some tea. We sat at the big oak table and drank silently. The room was warm and peaceful. Tom's old wooden armchair was at the table, where he'd eaten at midday. Everything was in order, ready for a new day. It was midnight, and I tried to get my mind to comprehend. Everything but this one, impossible fact became clear.

So I talked to the young policeman, early twenties, kind, deeply embarrassed. I said politely: "Do you often have to do this, tell people things?" And then, because the numbness was just starting to wear off and the first shimmer of pain coming, inevitably, in the distance: "Please, sit with me for a bit and let me talk to you".

I wanted a barrier of words for a while, so that I could feel by degrees and not all at once.

Time Out of Mind

Tom had left us around teatime. He had been minding our little girl, Esther, all afternoon while I was out teaching. He just said see you later, and went for the train. It was a celebration in London. A crowd of friends from the art college were going up to a private view of Daniel's paintings. They were planning to have a meal and then all come back together on the train. They must be on it, still. Somehow, *he* wasn't.

Suddenly I wanted to be alone. When that pain came I wanted to be by myself, and I knew that was how I could do it. I would not hide it but contrived to be alone, and then would feel that pain, and give myself to it, body and soul. So I said, "Goodnight, now – I'll go and ring up a friend and ask her to come and stay the night here. I know it's late, but she'll come".

The door shut after him, and I stood in the hall. The house so quiet, unharmed, and my mind travelled around it visiting each room; the three boys in the attic, one of them almost a man, and the little girl here in the room beside me. All his too. He couldn't harm them alive. So why should his death destroy anything? It would be different, the route. I pictured a tree, branching, and a great fork of the tree torn off in a storm, and the sap of the tree rising and flowing more strongly in other branches, restoring the balance. The same tree.

I'd stood for some time, I think, and then my head was very clear, and I went to our sitting room upstairs and phoned people. Before long the kitchen was full. All the friends off the train from Waterloo, and their wives, a dozen folk. We drank tea and tried to piece the events together. It was like some stage managers discussing the plot of a play, acting out the parts here and there. I was just the audience. When it was over I was going to be alone. I knew I had to get right through that first real fear of being alone, and it was just around the corner. They left about three a.m. Jan and Wynn stayed to sleep in the house.

> I sat in the lowest place
> Pierced, lacerated, sliced ...
> Myself, slavering orgasmic rain
> Crumbling my bowels like a wet shit.
> I'd said goodbye and thank you
> Politely enough, eyes dry

Fugue

But somewhat wide, not fighting tears
But weeping them inside
(I wanted to piss them wildly).
The voice stays steady,
Words sound cool and clear.
Within, the clamorous image kicks, knocking
Beating the mind to pulp.
It's a sandwich
Raw mince in the middle,
Oddly enough, underneath
Is as cool and clear as the top.
A voice then (whose?)
Sounding the distance, saying
Wait for me, love,
I will come ... back

For the second time that evening I went into our bedroom and closed the door. This was it. I had left the night lamp on over the bed. It threw an arc of light there, and I felt terribly cold inside, quite empty. I got into bed and turned out the light, pulled the sheet up over my head.

Flung one arm out into that space beside me. We'd always slept like two spoons in a drawer, and slept like logs, turning over together in one intuitive movement. For several minutes it seemed I was floating quite detached from myself, watching and waiting. Instinctively I turned on my side and was instantly caught, locked in a convulsive movement of body and mind, as if the soul would be spewed out in a helpless agonizing vomit, quite animal, beyond reason or faith, utterly abandoned to the dark ecstasy of grief. So close the borderline of the edges of experience that I felt relief in this strange impulse of love and immediately fell deeply asleep.

I woke very early. It was March and grey. Thursday's child was full of woe. Thursday. I waited until the boys were awake and then asked them to come into our room. I felt like someone else talking. The words came out of my mouth. I was listening too. Two covered their faces and wept silently, solemnly.

The other left the room without a word and went back to bed. He came back an hour later, fully dressed and ready for school. "I'll be going to school now", he said, and went. He was tireless, always preferred action to inaction. His room was full of experiments and gadgets of all kinds. Jonas.

Then I lifted little Esther out of her cot, her face rosy with sleep, and carried her into my room. She was radiant; brown curls, merry brown eyes. We sat, the four of us, and warmed ourselves at this glowing hearth. The two boys went to find breakfast, and I took Esther into the bed.

"Where's Tom?" (All his children called him Tom, not Dad)

"He's not here now".

"Why?"

"His heart went wrong, stopped beating. His body won't work anymore. He's dead".

"Will he come tomorrow?"

"No, but look, I'll put his clothes on. See, I'll wear them for Tom".

I got a shirt and a sweater and pulled them on – put his slippers on too. "Look, they fit me. He won't be here, and I'll wear them for him, and then you'll know he's really here, inside me. Part of him went away, but part of him will never go away. It's always here, and when we talk about him or think about him we'll know that. So I'll be Tom now, and you will be Tom, and then Rueben, Jonas, and Joseph will be Tom, and we'll wear his clothes for him and eat food and go to work and even learn to drive the car for him".

The days went by; relatives and friends came and went. At regular intervals I felt that astonishing animal convulsion, almost like an incipient sneeze, and I would tear out of the room to any empty space I could find, often enough the lavatory – the connection was not lost on me – where I could spew out my grief. Once Esther caught me at it. She came over, her small hands up to my face. "Why are you doing that?"

I told her, "I'm not used to having Tom inside me. It hurts".

"Yes", she said. "I'll love you better – I'll do it for Tom".

She climbed up on my lap and helped me to cry softly. "Come and see my new pussy-kittens now".

Fugue

The day of the funeral came, and Jonas decided, practical as ever, to be about his father's business that day. He set up a beer-making operation, and while the guests were having their tea and sandwiches, he wove his way through the crowded kitchen carrying steaming vessels of malt and hops. Completely preoccupied and determined, he measured and poured and stirred. An unmistakable brewery odour pervaded the house, and several people giggled happily. Later at supper, those who remained sat round and told ribald stories about Tom – and remembered the poem I'd read for him and indeed for dead Dylan too ... "And Death Shall Have no Dominion".

School holidays, and an invitation came to go to Scotland. We were to stay in a real castle (actually, it was a Victorian one). A vast house in a beautiful wild valley bordered by unbounded miles of moorland and hill, brown in the Easter sunshine. Sea loch and the blue-distant island of Mull. It was a journey to the Promised Land. I felt like Peter walking on the water, and I didn't sink. Every day was bliss. I was only aware of joy, an ebullient feeling of lightness, my heart lifted like the great sailing clouds out over the islands. Every tree, every movement of water and spray was radiant to me, and I was suddenly, inexpressibly in love. It was as if loving Tom had made it possible to love all persons. Each human being I came to was profoundly beautiful to me, each day a vibrating, vivid delight. The Isle of Rùm in the dark blue sea was darker than violet the mountains, sky and water bright as crystal in the April sun. The boys and Esther were rosy cheeked from wind from the highlands. Felix too. He was our adopted older son, 21 and rapier-minded. Kept the flow of words lively. We wrestled with them light-heartedly; had visions and theories, welded the world together as we walked and tirelessly scrambled the rocks on the almost uninhabited seashore.

> Islands there are in that indigo sea
> Sleeping shoulders humped to the wind
> Calling seals below, the swooping falcon
> Seeing all, as the rocks stand
> Steady in the swinging surge
> No past, no future, but now
> Time never was, nor number.

> In the scented grass,
> Sedges and heather,
> Comes care-less, sunshiny weather
> In spring, brown butterflies
> Flaunting the furze, and small brown feet
> Through the fragrant ferns
> Treading a path out, free from harms.
> No adder's bite or hornet stings
> Can threaten here
> Where Ardnamurchan sings

And now came thoughts. I'd been a person to think and know myself thinking. Something was different. A thought would be there, like the sound of a bell, and higher, ringing on and on. – "All things work together, Jo" – always I was being addressed as if by another voice, not mine. "A little child shall lead". These were familiar sayings, but they had pungency and determination in them that commanded complete attention. I felt, like the Hebrew boy Samuel, compelled to attend, to obey.

By now we'd left the hills and the becks, travelled the length of the land back to the South Coast and home. The same old home, the same good feeling of coming back to the familiar well-loved bit of living space. Tom's pipe smoke lingered somewhere. But it was changed.

Yes. Or rather, I was.

A layer, as if my conscious mind was peeling off, exposed another, deeper level. What it contained, that deeper area, I did not guess or even that such a process was beginning.

I had a dream. Not the everyday dream that you scarcely remember, that drifts lazily out of mind within a few minutes of waking, but a vision of such immediate intensity that I was instantly wide awake. Very simply, Tom came in through the open door of the room and stood leaning against the wall. Every detail was sharp, in focus, the sense of his reality, his actual presence, dynamic, overwhelming. My heart had leaped like a shooting star, the love I felt glowing like the billion suns in a spiral nebula. Ringing in my ears, again bell-like, not strident, but strong, I heard (and it seemed that it was me shouting out loud), *"It's a resurrection!"*

Fugue

> I woke today when the clock struck seven.
> Seven sharp bells were in my head.
> I dreamed that I had been in heaven
> Having this day my daily bread.
> You came to me there, my love, my love,
> In garments old, my King of Kings,
> Rough jersey and old trousers on,
> Warm hands instead of crown and wings.

The doctor had given me sleeping pills. I'd taken them obediently for about two months. I hadn't dreamed much.

Now I began to wake early, at three or four each day, and would get up and go in the kitchen and sit there; and a vast dream arose in my head of a new order of life, based on spontaneity of action rooted in love; and this must be guided by following some clues embedded in the growth process in the fundamental nature of things. I felt those two injunctions had to be followed explicitly, taken literally.

One morning my washing machine stopped working, I couldn't see why. Everything was plugged in. I started to work it out by the new route. Things working together, not just people and minds and organic structures. So I said, "What other thing have I to do that I have not done?"

So I went to find Esther, and her nappy was wet. I changed her, talked to her, and brought her with me into the kitchen.

"Will the washing machine work now?"

"Yes", she said.

I set the dial, and it started turning at once. Again the bell in my head sounded. "When two or three are gathered together".

Esther and I were gathered.

> To watch the ways of a child
> Is a world with wings?
> Marvel at mind making itself
> Like the wind that sings.
> Every gesture and sound is a song,
> Every impulse a speech,

> All movement a message immortal,
> Imprint of the all for the each.
> Follow the innocent fancy
> 'Kissing each thought as it flies',
> The children will give us the Kingdom
> As a surprise.

I decided then and there that from now on there were no coincidences but rather a gathering in the pattern of the process. Life was not a muddle but in fact a very complex order. I also at that moment remembered something else. Weeks back I had used the machine to dye some white submarine sweaters for the boys.

Esther had made a game out of it and had enjoyed the sound of the word dye. "Dye-dye-dye", she chanted. And for added effect: "Daddy-dye-dye, Daddy, dye-dye".

She laughed and chanted, sitting on the edge of the worktop, surveying her short legs and drumming her heels on the cupboard door. I heard her, really heard her. And set aside the flashing complex pattern of images that the words made in my head. Two weeks after that he was dead. She had told me. And in that depth of awareness where words are born, I had comprehended her.

We'd had a visiting lecturer from the art college, a brilliant young biochemist. He talked about DNA, the basic structuring ladder of life, built into every living organism, precisely determining its growth, the egg and the sperm, even before their union. Uniquely equipped for future forms. So thoughts are not separate from this process, I thought. The process is always unfolding, working itself through to the surface. Esther's tongue moving, innocent, wholly unmindful, expressed something 'beyond'; her spontaneous impulse to the present moment, like the DNA molecules impulse to imprint every cell with precise forms for the next stage of development, already contained the future, which is seeded in the present.

When I said, a month ago, "I don't understand", there was an echo at the back of my mind, like a name you can't remember, that I *did* understand. Or rather the hint that sometime later I would. "Now I see in a glass darkly, but then ..."

Fugue

The past and present whipped together as the washing machine tumbled and turned.

I stepped out of my previous view of myself and my environment like taking off a dress. I couldn't help myself. Something had peeled off again. It was unavoidable, something I knew which I couldn't un-know. It meant I couldn't ever again see life as separateness, but that every event of each moment, moving perpetually into the next was a connectedness; and that meant *everything*; from the furthest star to the sound of a cat meowing outside, or my fridge starting to pump. Things, people, electricity, magnetics, plants, animals. Yes, I constantly noticed that my thoughts were 'punctuated' by events outside. The mind and the outside connecting. There were sequences or runs of connection, sometimes comic, but often very frightening. No sooner had I become aware of punctuation than my scooter front tyre was *punctured* (daft). (What did you expect? This is all about being daft.)

> As cats may look at kings, and men at queens,
> Though many days must pass and come again,
> As mind and heart and limb have many scenes
> And girls to women change with might and main,
> Thus sing I, songs of silly strength
> Shrinking a while from all the paths I see
> Soothsaying, laid upon my length,
> As yardstick on a tailor's bench may be,
> Full fearing yet the shears that cut the cloth
> So fully longing that the robe will shape
> Its glory, and its damask love about
> My quaking body, navel, breast, and nape,
> Now through the rim of water runs my eye
> Our primavera shell will learn to fly.

I went to my teaching job, mornings, on my scooter and endured four miles of jam-tight traffic and very tricky driving. The man at the garage recommended a new tyre. Fair enough!

"Ready by the time we close".

I collected the scooter happily at five thirty and rode it to work next day. Another thing was happening. About two months had now passed since Tom abandoned his body, and mine. I'd been without him before, when he was a student at Ruskin College. At the end of the term he would come, and it was like Bunyan's celestial welcome, with sex thrown in, more golden than even he could imagine.

"Jo, it's amazing. We've been together like this for ten years, and just *see* what happens!"

> Understanding bursts like laughter
> Explode within the mind.
> Joy hatches out the fecund shell,
> Proclaims its vivid bliss.
> In every vein and nerve,
> Parades its pulsing perceptivity
> Within this kiss.

My body suddenly woke up. What had torn the heart now tore at my guts. I'd just fallen in love with the universe, but the universe didn't provide a body. I think it was possible that any tender, sincere man could have taken me into his arms at this time and relieved that rending hunger. It would have been a risk. I was in ecstasy of desire and despair. A consuming fantasy filled my heart and mind. It was that Tom's disembodied presence would manifest itself through the impulse of another being, who would act for him as I had acted in Tom's plan for my children. And I would accept that offering humbly and without demanding anything.

One day I asked two of Tom's friends to a meal, and before they arrived I had taken off my clothes and wrapped myself in a bedspread of many striped colours, like a child dressing up.

I was Joseph, but also Potiphar's wife. I fed my friends, and they knew I'd reached out beyond the limits of communication.

(My eldest son once played a trick on me. He had a new headphone set and bid me try it on, playing the Beatles song 'Let It Be'. The words and title were irresistible.

"Sing it", he said, watching closely. I sang out willingly, loudly, and noticed at once a change of expression on his face. A small smile opened in his cheek, and then a larger one. I sang a little louder. He began to laugh! I took off the headphones, saying "What's going on?" He told me, giggling, "Ma, you sounded like a cat on a roof, such a yawking and wailing. You thought you were singing the tune, but you couldn't hear yourself, so what came out was totally unlike what you thought *we* could hear – no song, but a caterwauling of meaningless noise".

"But the music was so clear in my head!" I protested. Without the connecting link with the outside sound, the inside sound could not be expressed or understood.)

In just this same way there was a message but no interpreter. I was talking a symbolic language, like an actor in a mime, a '*no*' play. Letters to a friend away became intense and fervent. The cry for help was louder, but the impression it made got fainter. I was writing to him in one of my night watches. The kitchen was warm and still but for two kittens who were rollicking around Esther's rocking horse. An extra sound caught my ear. They were slithering across the polished lino, chasing and scattering some small object. I got up to look. As I did so I heard a curious vibrating sound, like rattling teeth. I couldn't make out what. I looked round the room, trying to identify and locate it.

Then higher up on the shelf of the old Welsh dresser, eye to eye, I was looking at the skull. A young stag, found in a stream in Scotland. Lovely curving antlers. I was rooted to the spot, and the empty holes of its eyes melted into the space behind mine. I felt cold, and an electric shiver went through my body, almost sexual. I was afraid. I turned back to the kittens. The skull was still vibrating against the dresser. I picked up their toy. It was a domino. I'd seen it before, on the dresser shelf, a day or two before. Number nine, a four and a five. Before I could defend myself I was shattered by a stream of thoughts and mind pictures. Like a film with a very lively sound track. Nine: the day Tom died. May, the fifth month, and the fifth was Monday. "Four days". That was the title, the rest of it went like this, at tremendous speed.

It is lunchtime, and I am driving down through Franken, Victoria Road, and the Y-fork by the police station.

Time Out of Mind

Alberta Road. Just then my friend Margaret comes out of the back entrance of a house by the little post office and runs across the street without looking. I put on my brakes, sharply, to avoid hitting her, and feel myself catapulted through the air in head-over-heels flight, straight through the plate-glass front of the post office. For a fraction of a second I see a severed hand and both feet.

Silence …

I was dizzy and shaking, standing in the kitchen. I lifted up the lid of the Aga Cooker and put the kettle on. The Aga was like a household god, a reassuring, unbiased friend. I leaned against its warmth for a moment to regain my equilibrium.

This dream, this death-scene, was still fixed vividly in my mind. I was utterly convinced of it as an actuality.

I drank my tea and then with a characteristic practicality, I began to be busy. It was about two a.m. Time didn't matter anymore. I went to the bedroom and put all Tom's clothes into bundles for Oxfam. I pulled out the bed from the wall and searched underneath it for rubbish. Got all my dirty washing and put it in the machine. I was thorough, and intended to get everything in order. Then I sat down and wrote some letters, airmail for relatives and friends abroad, and put them ready on the dresser. They said, without preliminaries, that I would not be here after Monday, fifth of May. When I'd done that I'd had enough. I got my sleeping pills and shook the bottle. A heap of pills fell out on my palm. I felt compelled to take them all, because that was the way it happened. I would do that. It was rather a lot.

I woke late feeling very heavy. It was Saturday morning – I didn't get up. The front doorbell rang. I got up then, rather drunkenly, and opened it. It was Daniel, Tom's friend. I asked him to come in, to sit on my bed and talk. I told him everything, quite clearly I think, and without hysteria of any kind. He didn't say much, and left quite soon.

An hour later my doctor called. "Your friend rang – he said you were ill".

Fugue

"No, I'm not ill. But something will happen – I will be killed in an accident on Monday, on my motor scooter. I want you to help the kids. It's not suicide or anything. I just know it's true, it's real".

The scooter was out in the backyard. I could see it vividly in my mind, a rather battered grey Lambretta (O Lamb of God, who taketh away). It seemed important to get this dying business over with, as if it would put something right.

I wasn't sure what. It was like an assignment – a thing I had to do – or be. The doctor gave me some pills and left. I got an easy lunch together for the kids and didn't say much to them. The doctor came back. He asked me a lot of questions, and I gave him truthful answers, not hiding any of my thoughts, and he announced that I was to be taken to hospital. It sounded like a prison sentence, but I was feeling courageous (that was part of this 'play' I was in – I knew the part and how I had to do it). I couldn't get out of this part, though I wanted to cry out, "Stop, I want to get off here!" I just had to keep going and be wherever it took me.

I got some clothes, my nicest ones, my old red dressing gown, a kind of caftan, and climbed into the ambulance. Daniel promised to take care of the kids. Everything seemed inevitable. I was still sure about Monday ... even when I was put in a locked ward and given heavy doses of the antipsychotic drug Largactil.

I planned in my mind an escape – how I would break a window and walk through the street, in my red robe if need be. I felt incredibly restless, and my mind raced faster and faster as the Largactil slowed up my body movements. On Sunday, another patient, a beautiful, slender girl of about 20 plunged through a plate-glass window, lacerating her face and body. She was crisscrossed with stitches from head to toe. They boarded up the window, and I then discovered that the windows were of double thickness and would only open four inches at top or bottom. I felt caged in and had a deep queasy feeling in my stomach; real fear. But I didn't know why I was afraid. I began to look for something real to be afraid of.

Monday came and went. I felt like a child who has got up late and is afraid to go to school, slinks round the house hoping no one will see. I began to draw the patients. I was trying to find Tom in their faces. My

Time Out of Mind

hands and feet were like lead, every movement an effort to counter the effects of the drug. I drank gallons of water in an attempt to wash the stuff out of me. But I drew, even when my fingers were so weak they couldn't grip the pencil. Bell-like thoughts again, the old sayings, faint but clearer than the sky when the first star appears, and as small a sound as that silver pinpoint of light in the violet dark. "Perfect love casts out fear". Perfect love, perfect love, perfect love. The bell sounded and faded into an infinite ocean, a vast canopy of space. I searched everyone's face for that perfect love – and saw it, imperfect. I couldn't comprehend it, but I felt it. Feeling ... how could I feel?

The doctors asked me to sit with them and some other people, students, caseworkers, nurses, and such, and answer some questions. It was a sort of tribunal. I began to tell them about Tom and how I would not have met him but for Vic, my brother-in-law, and how I would not have met Vic but for my own brother, Charles, who'd been killed in Burma in the war. And I talked, and I loved these people. I began to weep tears upon tears with all those people watching, and I was stuck in a chair, like an interview for a job, and they just watched me, and I told them about love and the tears soaked into my collar.

I kept looking for somewhere, someone who would take some of the love I felt; it was like cooking food for a party and no one wanting to come and eat it. People on the ward said I was arrogant, opinionated. I started to work instead of talk, to listen a bit.

> My hymn is silence, and my prayer is dumb,
> I may not sing or speak my love until he is come.
> My body utters words, my heart cries out,
> My tongue is still, yet my soul will shout
> Thoughts come in purple robes to deck the mind.
> I send them forth again my love to find;
> Fervent ambassadors, they greet him in the dark
> And break the locks and chains around his heart

I felt heavy like lead with Largactil, a terrible lethargy. Body and mind were desperate for relief – no exercise or fresh air, all locked up. And fear. One morning I woke as usual at five a.m. I got up and began

Fugue

to do exercises until I could feel some sensation through all that drugged haze. I decided I would take no more pills.

When the queue formed I joined it. I said, "I won't take any more pills until I've seen the doctor".

I hadn't seen a doctor for ten days. I felt elated, high.

During the day a curious lightness in the head and limbs, as if no part of the body really belonged to me, might just float off any moment, leaving me without legs or arms or brain even.

The thinking part of myself detached and glided out from the rest on a long thread of time and space, and that thread, like an elastic, felt more and more tension and tightness. Meanwhile there were thoughts, dreams.

I was acutely wide awake, every impression sharply recorded, keenly felt. The whole nervous system was tuned up – a maximum tuning in every receptive faculty. A recurring theme, which had accompanied me ever since I found myself in a locked ward – rescue. I dreamed of it, I looked for it, I expected that somehow rescue would come. A man, a Tom in another form, would come and take me out of this alien place. He'd love and embrace me, and we'd go together to some new delightful home. He would love and nurture my children too, and we'd all work and live together – happily ever after.

I'd become so sure this would be true, not a dream. I felt overwhelming hope that a friend in far-off Wales would come in his car and fetch me. Werner was a refugee from Nazi Germany, a journalist and writer. *Now*, he was setting out, *now*, drawn to help me, knowing by some deep intuition of love that a new life would grow from dung of disaster. I reached for him in my mind, willing him to come. Blazing with hope like the star in the East. The afternoon came. I felt intolerably alone. Consciousness swung near and far on that fragile stem, and my head swam and extended like a bubble blown by a child. I fumbled, trembling with fingers that would not respond. They belonged to someone else, like the tongs a nuclear physicist has through the glass when he handles radioactive substances. My purse, some coins for the phone. I'd ring him. They let me get to the phone box, and I got the right number. His voice, gentle as always, with its subtle foreign accent, slightly sing-song.

He reproved me. "It's not good for you to talk, and I cannot talk to you; I'm not good on the phone. You must go back to your own self, discover in silence the dark places of your identity. Talking will only conceal and make a barrier. Don't try to hide your truth by talking. Just give yourself up to the experience of being what you are!"

> This is the marching month, the battlefield,
> The Waterloo time, the deadly doubting time.
> The veteran private feels his old wound in his private parts.
> Smart, the memory of fiery trial does not depart.
> Corporal now, the incarnated soul of the once King
> Sits like a meditating cat, waiting to leap,
> Dies of fright, actually, at each bullet's flight
> And incarnates again to face the next –
> Come, Poor Ole Joe, don't fret;
> The battle will be done, and heaven is yet.

I walked back to the ward and went to my bed. I lay on my back with the grimy hospital ceiling glaring down at me. My star of hope went out, and I was left with that bubble of my mind, expanding and spinning, a membrane stretched to perilous tightness and thinness. I lay until night came. No sleep, only this endless unbearable awareness, as if consciousness itself could extend to the limitless edges of time and the universe.

The light came in at the high window; the wall beside me slowly focused into colour. I got out of bed. My legs, my whole body felt leaden, heavy, sodden, a sack of molasses. I went to find a chair in the dayroom, steering my way through the furniture and the people, a car with four punctures. Day had begun, meals and pills and nurses.

"Come along now, Mrs Thomas, make sure you swallow them".

I had to join this line again and say my bit about no more pills.

"You're being very silly, dear. You come here to get well, you should accept the treatment!"

"Will the doctor see me today"?

"Yes, of course. Today".

I went back to my chair, each step needing all my will, just to lift a foot clear of the ground. Towards later afternoon I began to gasp, like someone drowning. The bubble had reached its limit. Every piece of my skin crawled and prickled with a kind of electric intensity. I didn't feel physically sick but began to retch, the huge gasps alternating with a rigidity that clouded every muscle and made it difficult to breathe. A nurse came and another patient, Dawn. She held my hand. I tried to speak. A rasping voice came out, animal, alien. "It's a tension, a tension, a tension … I can't, *I can't, I* can't". A convulsion …

("Jesus, Jesus, come to the beach. We're going to play on the beach!" Kids, laughing, clean shorts in the cool dawn, clean air shimmering brightly with a young sunshine, risen minutes ago with long light on white sand, the sea immaculate, deeper than blue, hazing into the horizon. Such a space of white sand, smooth like new snow; golden in the rays of the sun, higher now. The wind blowing deliciously fresh, rippling on the skin, crisp crimple of sand particles between the toes.

Yes, yes, I'm coming – c'mon … let's run. We run, swooping arms out, like swallows, leaping and laughing, breath a perfect expanding of ribs and lungs, drawing in gulps of air, weaving in intricate patterns leaving a trace on the sand with many intersections.

"Jesus, your legs are so long, wait for us! A little cart is there, a small wiry pony, bright grey with a white mane. Jesus runs, puts on the skies, a new game. The ponies swing round in a huge curve, fast as the breeze. Jesus is like a bird skimming the mirror of wet sand, aquaplaning, singing, then a swift movement like spitting, something flies out from the head, shoots across the water flicking the surface, a profound stillness of shock. There on the sand lies a skin, just a skin, an empty bladder, body-shaped with the head end an open orifice, a hole puncturing the smooth satin surface. Silence of wind and sand and no shouting.)

Convulsion. A deep retching sob shoved its way to the surface. It felt as if the chest was splitting open, as if an axe had sunk halfway and the mind and body were slowly cracking apart. Huge shudders came; they seemed never-ending. I felt another patient's hand and Nurse Turner's, and held on (I knew they were there). Then, harsh croaking sobs came with each breath; dry, so dry. They pulled me onto the bed and I lay on my back. Silence at last and the tears fell. Tension and tightness flooded away in the wetness, oh, the ease of it. Lying flat, I cried, very quietly and effortlessly; all the stress oozed out of me, streamed away in the flow; all that had been harsh was tender now.

Too tender, I guessed. I'd got skinned, and how would I live without it? I didn't know. I suspected there was more to come. Another stage that I hadn't thought existed.

"Perfect love ..." Since that day, when my mind had opened so strongly to that thought, I had begun to feel my body again. All sensation had died with the thought of death. Now, as summer came, I felt the old warmth. Visits from the children reminded me of Tom as a physical fact. I felt a new kind of separateness from him, as if he were a spiritual fact and I was a physical fact. I was searching for a way to unite these two things. Only one way; I must do it myself. The ancient prohibitions hovered in my head, and vied with the words I kept hearing, I set thoughts aside and abandoned myself to my own physical fact, which blossomed within as richly as ever in the past. I'm wearing Tom's coat for him, I had told Esther, buttoning up the wooden toggles on his old black duffle. I was Tom's hands for him, and when the climaxes came, I was his head as well, full of golden light.

> Months of time since you left your body and mine –
> Yes, four months gone.
> I've seen you many times since then in other men's flesh,
> Dwelling yourself.
> Self of myself, seeking a soul to receive you
> Took mine.
> Together we, the matrix of our conjoined selves,
> Are seekers still –

> Body and soul searching the eye to eye
> Our thou to find
> Until we shall see Him face to face
> And mind to mind.

I felt renewed, reassured. "All shall be well, and all manner of things shall be well".

But no one else knew what was happening. I saw a doctor, at last. I told him I'd stopped taking the Largactil. He looked a bit displeased but said nothing.

"It's all right, Mrs Thomas; we're going to treat you in another way – I want you to have six ESTs, electrical therapy".

"But I feel better!"

"This treatment will be useful and you should have it".

I watched batches of patients going for this treatment. They had the bewildered, hopeless look of people caught in a pogrom. Very, very few could accept it with equanimity. The majority were deeply afraid, even when in control. Patients who refused to cooperate were spoken to sharply, like naughty children, and they often burst into tears. Tension would mount and patients spread rumours and horror stories about what could happen. No one explained anything properly. It was a mystery, a nightmare. I began to be infected by these fears; one fact of the treatment was that during the electrical convulsion (hadn't I had enough of my own?) the patient bit heavily with a clamping movement of the jaw. A rubber gag was placed between the teeth to prevent the tongue being bitten through. (I remembered that a child, a cousin of mine, had bled to death after biting his tongue.) A nurse prepared these gags, binding them with cotton wadding. They had to be made strongly. No one knows quite why EST is useful. The electromagnetic function of the brain is stimulated, affected some way, and the patient begins to be forgetful, not of the important things but of small details. The other thoughts continue, but at a slower pace, and a 'pause' is created in the processes of the mind. Some intensity of focus is lost, and also some concentration and feeling. (I went to see a few films during this period and cannot remember the content of any of them.) Anyway, it makes the patient quieter.

I was sure, every time they proposed to do this to me, that I would die. The anaesthetic needle pierced my skin, and as my brain fogged over I said some sort of goodbye. A spinning sequence of green willow trees along the fen waysides, no panic, tears, or pleading. Some fear and some willingness. *"Unless the seed fall into the ground"*. The words again, bell-like in my head. Waking was painful. The head would ache; everyone was lying on beds pushed very close together, like fish on slabs. It was some kind of conservatory area, with a glass roof. The June sun beat down. Slowly, a sense of time and place came back. Toes could wriggle, eyes blink. A cup of hot coffee.

"Come along, Mrs Thomas, sit up and drink this!"

I was back.

>Small things frighten me, I fear,
>Driving between two lorries, even minis, in a narrow street,
>Doing a hill-start at a traffic light
>With tailgating cars streaked out behind
>Or the darkness in the garage just before
>I turn on the light.
>As I carry out the rubbish for the dustbin men
>Sometimes a sharp ring on the doorbell,
>The unexpected visitor (no, it's one of the boys),
>The very idea of fire, which of all things
>I love most,
>A little sharpness in a woman's words wilts me for a while
>Or criticism, even small
>Which makes me cry like a child – afterwards.
>So I will love my fear, I swear;
>The narrow space, the hill (I have my skill),
>Dark shadows yet to be illumined and
>The stranger, above all the unexpected
>Event,
>Harsh words are but the sanding when
>The craftsman fines his work to smoothness,
>Showing the grain and gloss;

> Finally fire, oh fearful friend!
> Be thankful that you fear it,
> For that is your natural shield.
> Fire will never make you shrink,
> For fire cannot consume fire

I had the whole series of treatments without ever being told why or what was happening. One aspect of fear is ignorance. (A thought unbidden, floating, untethered, hovering in my mind *"Perfect love"*. *"Oh God, Tom, I love you".*)

That evening I was in the washroom. Many basins and three baths in a row with a curtain rail between. An old lady in a wheelchair needed some help. I washed her feet; she was arthritic and was unable to reach them. I then cleaned a couple of messy hand basins. It was getting dark, and the place was very quiet, warm. I stayed after she'd gone and looked in the mirror. Short-cropped hair, 42, not a pretty fact. I had on the old red robe. A masculine alter ego seemed to hover there. I knew myself as a man, dimly felt that I could know, or had known what being man was; a real experience.

I said aloud, "I wish I could feel sex like a man feels it".

The lights fused, and everything went black. I shuffled around in the dark, trying to find the door; out into the main ward, where some faint light came from outside, up the centre between the lines of beds, into the corner next to the padded isolation ward, and found my own small room. I shut the door, pulled the little curtain close over the observation window, and climbed onto the bed. Very dark, very peaceful. I lay on my back, hesitant, in a half listening state, could hear my heart, my head humming gently. The darkness wrapped around me like a protecting membrane, and words came, utterance of ancient immeasurable depth, softer than sound, more subtle than thought, clearer than any describable note, un-played, unspoken, unfolded. The impulse to respond was beyond the mind, eager, inevitable.

Tom's hands were mine, my body his, it had always been his, and was never more so than now. I opened myself, abandoned to whatever body and mind could feel and flow in this unity. Sensation unfolded petal by petal; sparkles and flakes of gold light scattered the path of consciousness, a bright glowing tension filled the breast, ardent, expanding until, in like manner, the vulva flowered in a brilliant cascade of warmth and was illumined like the sun. My eyes, closed in the dark, my mind turned inward to the light. Awareness, total, consuming at this moment, aroused, astonished as a brilliance of light flooded the eyelids from the outside. At precisely the moment when brightness within was at its greatest intensity, the fuse was mended, and all the hospital lights suddenly turned on together. I opened my eyes, dazzled. Shut them again quickly. My heart was beating strongly, every nerve fiber a blessing. I was satisfied. I was whole – *holy*. It was an annunciation.

> Rise, rise into the sky, ride high;
> My ship of space and time
> Is nigh, nearing the newness of
> A dawning dream come
> True.
> I am awake now, you woke me
> Love
> You came, bearing a gold symbol
> Seal of my soul, searing me.
> The crucible is full, the metal fine,
> The mould is shaped, prepared.
> Pour out now
> And bear it to the assembled guests.
> Drink all of you this gold,
> This wine of mine,
> Not servant now, but friend.
> The invitation open, free
> Returning I (promised it)
> Greet you, arms out wide,
> Wearing the stars in my belt, in my hair,
> In my eyes.
> Lord, I a door –
> Am, open at last, come in and through
> Triumphing, laughing,
> Singing, weeping, reaping
> This day's shine.

Alice was another patient. She was ancient, wrinkled with thousands of delicate lines, had a purposeful face with fine cheekbones and jaw, an aquiline nose. She would prowl round the wards at night, rummage in lockers, hide clothing and private articles away, to the fury of the other inmates. She never spoke or did anything else but sob silently in the dayroom day after day. I was drawing, mostly faces, and I drew her. She watched me, never speaking. I drew an outline picture, like in a child's drawing book. A cottage with flowers outside, a tree. A pathway to a gate. I handed it to her, and a box of pastels. She picked them up and began filling in the colours. Then she started to write all over it, in tiny flowing scrawl, a sequence of words forming a stream of patterns. It flowed all around the rooftop, over the tree, and up the garden path. Then, on to the back of the paper, I drew another picture, and another. She adorned them, and wrote more and more. Then she began to talk, to ask me to make special outlines. A table with a meal on it. Two chairs. A little girl dressed for a party. A bride. Once she took a head I had painted. It was a curious thing. A composite face drawn from life from three girls in the ward. The eyes of one, the nose of another, the mouth of the third, the outline was of my own. I called her Helena the Fair. She was a female Christ, the beautiful one, the anointed. Alice took the picture and encircled the head with a halo of her writing six lines deep. When she had finished she began talking, quietly and gracefully, about herself, her house, her children. She went out and tidied herself, did her hair. She never again made a nuisance of herself. She helped the other patients and began to talk to them too. She was well now, and I was well now, perhaps. For a time. It was as well …

I longed for the outside, for ordinary life. There were still ESTs to undergo. No one ever talked to me about how I felt, or what its effects were on me. In five weeks I had spent less than ten minutes with a doctor on three occasions.

A locked ward is an airless place. The beach, the sea, and the sky were less than a mile away. I begged a little, asked around, and surprisingly got permission to take a small group of women from the ward with me. Dylis came, and Katie, and about four others; we could go before breakfast, at seven. We all felt the exhilaration. Going out through the heavy doors to the sound of keys turning in the lock behind us. Out

Time Out of Mind

of the main gate, the long driveway. Past the semidetached villas, and the big pub on the foreshore, where we had so often been for a beer or to buy red mullet or sea trout from the Sunday fishermen. Then, cutting through the little wooden chalets and across the sandy grass, down on to the pebble shore itself, where the cool sea smell came like soma to our senses, and the gulls swooped and swerved, looking for fish.

Walking, not talking much. Returning past old boats half sunk in the estuary mud, and a rare fisherman stowing his gear after a night in the harbour. Hardly anyone about. Quiet, a lark singing somewhere, very high up.

Back in the ward, breakfast never tasted so good. We never even heard them lock the door; our heads were so full of the morning and birdsong.

Then, I don't remember how, I was home, no recollection of a moment of arrival, or some special detail. The whole picture swims and merges. Gleeful gossiping with the boys over secret beer-making in the attic while older relatives turned their scandalised necks, the warmth of motherly sisters and the big welcome back at my teaching job. Esther's merry 2-year-old talk, so joyous and chirruping, robin-like.

I took my scooter out into the road; enemy or friend? I felt slightly embarrassed, making a reconciliation with this image of fear, degradation, and pain. I felt I should make some apology; say something conciliatory and reassuring. Time for an MOT test. Spells TOM backwards. Like DOG and GOD. Better get it straight to the garage. It may take several days, and I need it for work on Wednesday.

> "To TEH – A Riddle"
> The greatest power in the universe is words.
> "Come forth", you said,
> And did.
> And I consider now my own,
> Wonder in deed at them,
> Their striving and duplicity,
> Their strength and dire simplicity.
> My mind (mind how you go)
> Takes words and plays

A thousand merry, mocking tricks
Whist you not that TOM is trumps?
Unseemly this, to unzip language.
Thus – *le mot* (as they say in French)
Is in the beginning
The English preposition bears the theme,
And many more besides
"TH". The link between. Above all
THE – the th'is, and th'at, the
O'ther th'ing, are th'us
Entwined.
Next take the form, the cruciform, the t of lower
case and childhood's script; when grown to man's
estate becomes the capital.
The head has lost his head, the piper's son
Whose topknot has blown off.
E is for Ernest, trident of triplicity – three-pointed
Arrow for endeavour and
Forever and ever and ever, world without end.
He is T'OM (Have you passed your MOT test?)
H is a cornerstone, a bridge between two *I*s, or *i*s, the yeses
Have it, and the H an open-ended A – the ass can hee and haw at
Last, for who lives longest
Laughs

I went to get my scooter on the Monday morning. I wandered through the smart shop where gleaming bikes stood in rows, shining flanks of steel and chromium, all colours. I left through the repair shop at the back, where black grease reigned, and spare parts littered the ground, the spilt intestines of many an engine crowding every corner.

The man wiped his hands on a rag and looked at me with unexpected intensity. "Have you been riding this? Recently?"

"Well, no. I've been in hospital".

"Did someone change the tyre?"

"Yes, actually, just a day or two before I went in".

"You can thank your bloody stars – if you'd ridden it, you'd most likely be dead. The way it was when you brought it in, it was a killer. Good thing the test came up before you could take it on the road again!"

"What's wrong with it?" My heart was beating a bit fast, and I waited for his answer like someone about to be told the solution to a baffling problem.

"You see, it's the front wheel. It's been put back on the wrong way round. This brake attachment here. Easy enough to put right, but the way it was, first time you put the front brake on hard, the cable would have wrapped itself round the wheel head and locked it. You'd have been catapulted over the top of the handlebars slap into whatever was there – let alone the road!"

"Yes, I see", I said. "Well, thanks a lot for testing it. OK now? Looks like I had a narrow escape".

"You can say that again".

I wheeled TWO 976 out in the lane and it started instantly. I've always enjoyed riding a scooter.

Durdle Door in Dorset. A summer outing with the kids – skin diving – my first in deep water. The pool a gleaming oval of turquoise. We swam out to the rocks where a cleft drops deep to the floor of the outer ocean, and dived down until our ears hurt. A splendour of shafted light intersected the cool green spaces filled with fronds of weed and fish moving and swaying in the rock of the waves. A daring dive into a light-filled hole, and then up, head out into a cave, the inside the door itself. Coming out, I saw Tom's watch still on my wrist. An hour in the sea. Oh well! I gave it him one birthday. It didn't go again.

We went camping in Cornwall a month later. Found a tiny cove, almost to ourselves. A minute patch of clean sand, shelving into gravel. A cluster of sharply pointed rocks and clefts, with the sea pounding into the cracks, gushing explosively as the tide pushed its way up the shore. The water here was clear as in a glass, the pebbles magnified in it, and their colours enhanced in the wetness. Rueben, with home-made wetsuit was diving again and again. Came out shaking the water from his mask and a look of private satisfaction in his eye.

"Mum, how about this then?" He held out his hand, fist clenched, and opened it slowly. In it was a stainless steel watch, no strap. I picked it up and turned it over. Self-winding, waterproof. It was going steadily.

"Back there, about ten yards out, in six feet of water. I saw it in the gravel. The light on the glass caught my eye".

We enquired in the village pub and post office if anyone had lost a watch. No one had. So I bought a strap, and Rueben wore it. It kept stopping, starting again.

"Come on, Mum", he said. "You have it – it doesn't go for me".

I put it on, and it stayed there for two years. It didn't stop until I emigrated to Chicago. It refused to go a few days after we arrived there. Just another of 'those', we said, getting used to it. My synchrometer. I suspect I'm getting to be one of Jung's archaic people.

(The outside and the inside were beginning to synchronise. The objective-subjective world of mind and body, being a person in this tiny patch of liveliness called 'a life', was becoming altered qualitatively by a new kind of experience. Or was the experience the same, the perception different? No, I don't think so. Both together. The degree of difference is important because in this new field of mind activity you could not help noticing things; the connections forced themselves upon you, the denouements unavoidable – like *Peanuts*, one kept saying Aaaaarh!)

Two years later, and I've lived a lively time, not dull; domestic, growth, kids growing and changing, a hopeful feeling in the heart, but an ache too, for that good, partnership in kind. Too much hope maybe. I longed for that far-flung rescue still, the one that I had so vividly imagined. It never came. But something did. An invitation to go to America, share a life with kinsfolk in Chicago; to leave sorrow behind and go to the New World, a new life, possibly a new partner. I was always an obedient lady – I'd have gone anywhere. It was enough to be asked – and I accepted joyfully.

I applied for a labour permit to work in the United States. That took nine months. I applied for a visa. Much more difficult, and a lot of pressure was put on me by the immigration department, probing into my past and Tom's, our left wing enthusiasms of sixteen years ago. But I persisted, determined that I would go. We all would go. It was a family adventure. The questions were intensive, and a visa was granted. Then it was withdrawn again. No reason given. I was sent for and further questions began; a sense of pressure. I felt I was being squeezed by a huge hand. I kept still inside myself and held on with Tom in my mind. I told a lot of lies. They asked those kinds of questions. I hated lying but couldn't help it. 'They' was a dignified intelligent public servant used to his authority. I felt some kindness there, under his piercing black brows. He kept Esther's passport photo on top of our file, looking at him with 4-year-old directness. My 44-year-old confusions grew less when I thought of her. Perhaps his did too.

I gave my notice and bought the tickets, arranged to sell the house and furniture. I knew the visa would come, but it might be a few weeks. It was nearly half term.

And quite suddenly, it was all happening again. The outside and the inside. That process begun in the shadow of death two years before began again now as if a dormant seed lying in the ground for a season was once again fertilised and seeking a new growth for itself. It was all spontaneous, inevitable – nothing could stop it, and I knew when it started – 'it' was me, my under/inner side …

> My time is not yet come
> You said the time before
> Coming and going you waited the hour
> The intuited moment of testing
> Trial of strength, titanic truth
> Telling.
> Here in my flesh you await me
> Self of myself, the rim and the core
> Sworn, sought and seeking
> Spurning naught, necessities wrought by
> Love above all, all of me
> Turned, tuned for the fire
> Funnelling forth, fearing, daring
> To focus, drawing the life and the light
> Down through the round lens of
> My body, my eye, ear, all senses
> Centring

Fugue

>Circle to circle, summarize
>Sunrise

I put myself in front of an attic window, in the full blaze of the morning sun, where the hot rays could pierce and penetrate, penis-like. The flame within echoed to the sky, warmth to warmth and sang out like a trumpet, a triumphal march. The hound of heaven – I fled him down the nights and down the days. It wasn't like that. I went to the Catholic priest, tears streaming down my face, and told him I was in love with God. I confessed it like a sin. Everything was inside out, the words, like in *Alice in Wonderland*, kept coming out wrong.

"I chased him through the days and through the nights. I chased him along the straight paths of my own body".

I was appalled, helpless. He absolved me and told me to be good.

>The queen's 'head' is up for sale,
>She's waiting.
>Oh God, it hurts, my head is aching,
>Belly too.
>I drank too many wines last night.
>It was fun,
>But food and wine are not for sale.
>Bought at enormous cost
>We eat and drink unbounded
>Free and bounding
>The strong, supple, suppliant body
>Fir treelike – evergreen,
>A yew
>Never dying, growing ring by ring
>Through paeans of time undaunted
>Though forests fall all;
>All it is
>And that is all

At home, a man, a stranger was coming to dinner. I had joined a marriage agency months ago, my sister's idea. They send some

Time Out of Mind

suggestions, but no meetings so far. Now I told them that I was going to America, and quite immediately an interview was forthcoming (£30 to pay). I was ready to believe that this man would be the rescuer. I cleaned the house; a friend came and helped to prepare a beautiful meal. I bought expensive flowers. The house was radiant.

He came at the expected time, a tall, broad-shouldered man with a deep voice and kind eyes. He was divorcing his wife, had lively kids, same ages as mine, wanted a new life. He'd had polio, and this had left him almost unable to walk. He had elaborate steel crutches to assist him, and he managed well. We ate and drank. We all enjoyed it. Esther too. He talked nicely and well, especially about music. Then he took me out in his car for a drive. It was a serene evening in late May. We drove out to the South Downs, through tiny leafy villages and up a chalky track. He stopped there and we talked, watched the sun, orange now, going down. A herd of young cows came nosing and snuffling to the fence, leaned over affectionately. I told him as much as I could and that I was probably mad, by the definition of the majority, at least. And he told me that he was not all that he seemed. I liked him, his easy kindness, and his honesty. He told me of how he fought to stay alive in an iron lung. And all the time my body glowed like the orange sun, a hidden fire, and I knew that I was in love, but not with him. I think he was included in this, part of its possessing me in that way, but he was not the whole, the agent of that wholeness. He turned my face towards him with one hand and kissed me very gently. Then he started the car and drove home. We did not talk. He had to go back that evening. I did not ask him in and went into the house.

It was Whit weekend. Friday and Sunday we were going on a week's travelling, all of us, in the VW bus visiting friends and family. Saturday was a day to prepare, iron some clothes and pack. Esther made a cake. I couldn't find a tin so we put it in a jelly mould and then into the Aga oven. You could make an atom bomb in an Aga stove if you knew the formula, someone had said. A-tom. Tom, oh Tom.

> I have a nickname for my soul
> Myself,
> I call him Tom.

Fugue

There is a silent space within
A silence, and we talk.
We fought there, once, he bullied
Baffled me, wanted burnt offerings, and got charred
Steak and onions from my cooking stove;
(Once dreamed I was another Jo, an Arch-type girl, a
Cinderella too)
To Tom I talk, old nick-Name friend,
He answers yes, yes Jo, I love you, Jo, and so I'll go
Along and anywhere
Across a universe or two
Drift with a comet's tail, dance
Seven veils of nebulae, go
Dabbling in galactic dew,
Rock to the slow pulse of a bright quasar, or else
Go shopping in the Albany Road
Buy cheese and veg and treats
For Esther (kids are playing in the rain).
Post Christmas letters in the rush,
Walk miles in Chicago slush,
Console a man who has no luck
Try pushing when the van is stuck
Whatever bidden, that I'll do
For Tom, I am in love with you.

I read to Esther, as often, from a Ladybird story book, her favourite, *Cinderella*. *Cinderella*, a story for kids. *A deep searing and prickling of fear.* I put Esther to bed and went back to my own room. *Cinders.* That's what the earth would be one day – again. Unless …? *Cinderella*; a vision, a film ran through my mind of unimaginably ancient times beyond recorded history, and many stratas deep in rocks when the earth was another earth, youthful and rash. I was Cinderella caught in the dark, in my rags, the coach and horses vanished, my prince a lost dream. Up through the dark layers of time and mind came a flash of doom. The stroke of midnight – her obedience to that stroke. On that depended her return to hearth and home. It all became here and *now*.

Time Out of Mind

There were four boys in the house, another lad was spending holidays with us. I gathered them round.

"Go to bed now, and don't come out of your rooms. You must be asleep early, before midnight. *It's very important.* You must be in your own room and stay there. If you disobey, the world will be destroyed. It's up to you".

On our domestic level of obedience – yes. Once before the earth had blackened and died in charred dust, fire within and fire without. Body ablaze, that was Joan of Arc, a human cinder – Jo an ark, yes an ark. This house, the boys, and Esther and I afloat with doors sealed … ashes and cinders …

> A curious shape in my mind, like a huge bottle, narrow-necked. It was in the ground, a hole dug in a coal seam, the opening narrow, wide enough for a man, a bottleneck. They were forcing a crowd of people into that hole, just pushing them into it, one at a time; they were desperately trying to claw their way out again. Clinging to the edge until their fingers were kicked. A churning mass of naked men and women at the bottom of the bottle, surrounded on all sides by the black shining coal.
>
> A bundle of loaves thrown down and a skin of water lowered on a rope. Someone tried to hold on as it jerked up again, but they cut it just as he got to the top. It's a matter of days now; they'll keep them alive like that. They never know when it will happen. The others, who are enjoying this sport, usually start the fire when the stench from below becomes unbearable. There are gutters cut in the side of the bottleneck, running deep into the cavity. When the time is decided, oil is poured into a specially built rim at the top, and as it runs down it trickles and flows over the coaly surface inside, a film which soon reaches the bottom. Four chosen men ignite the oil, which flares up into the sky, and then with amazing speed the flames trail their way into the

interior. The scream which comes forth from the mouth of the hole begins at once and rises to a pitch of shattering intensity – that one vibration of sound which those left above believe will balance the forces of nature in their favour. The silence which immediately follows is filled instantly with a vast subterranean roaring as the furnace of coal and flesh reaches its climax, a gigantic tongue of flame rising from the bottle neck as the vessel is gutted; but this time, the forces of nature, spontaneously releasing these energies, evolve in the vehemence of anger and fear, and in that fury of combustion, fission occurs; the rumble and roaring rise to a climax which splits the rocks into fragments, and for the first time on earth, a mushroom cloud rises to the atmosphere ...

The dream, if it was a dream, went on until daybreak. I felt as if I had not slept. The sky was a pale lilac – one star. I opened my door very quietly and heard Esther singing to herself. I went into the kitchen and looked at the Aga cooker. Minutes passed. I remembered the shape of the fire box inside. Bottle-shaped. I also remembered Esther's cake. I opened the oven and took it out. One jelly mould and one perfectly formed jelly-shaped cinder. It turned out beautifully and I put it on a pretty plate in the middle of the kitchen table. Gelignite? Something spoke in the back of ray head, very softly. Jo, it's all a joke; the whole thing is; *it's all a joke!* I began to giggle. I did actually believe it. (But the dream hung in my mind like a black taste, and I never forgot it.) Perhaps a memory dimly imprinted in the DNA came like a bubble to the surface. No wonder the mediaeval people were so impressed by the image of hell! (You must be joking.) The boys coming for breakfast, laughed like drains when they saw the jelly on the table.

A week later (it seemed months) I went to the College of Art to look at an exhibition of third-year work. Dip. One student was exploring jellies. There was a series of pictures, paintings, engravings, collages; rows and rows of jellies, that same moulded shape, every texture and colour you could think of. "'Mother Nature!" I said to myself. "Just what is going on?"

Time Out of Mind

The eve of Pentecost. I laid the table for supper. We were going on a journey in the morning – a magical mystery tour, as the latest Beatles song was telling us. A last supper – last? Before what? I made lamb curry; that would be right, a Paschal Passover lamb, and put a round roll at every place, like the ones Leonardo's paintings portrayed. I broke up a roll of bread and passed it around rather hurriedly, wanting to get it over and done. Then a glass of water – we didn't have any wine. Bread and water – that was a symbol of affliction wasn't it? We ate the curry somewhat hastily too, as if we had to be going, although we were not setting off until nine the following morning. I felt restless, energetic, as if some tremendous event would occur.

I finished the preparations for the journey. Esther was asleep, and the boys were in the attic watching telly. I began to have a strong urgent, vivid desire – my bowels were turned out like water – heart and body panting after the waterbrooks. This love, this fervent, amazing inevitable love. I made love to this love, opened my body and mind wide as the sky. Tom was in this love, and so was I, but I lost myself there, shot to the stars in impulses of energy. This, this is the impulse which moves the galaxies – the turning worlds and the spinning electrons ... the whole evolution of nature in this. Time was no time at all. The orgasm spread like the rays of the rising sun, enveloping every nerve ending in pulsations of light. I heard a great cry, which filled the room, echoing in my head, and again, again. JES -US- CHRI-ST. I heard someone gasping, breathless. The cry and the breath had both been mine after all. It was a consummation, a covenant, newly made. I wasn't sure how, or what it was all about, except that it had to do with Tom. Thoughts began to drift – I lay down to sleep. That dream, that resurrection, that rescue. It was real; it would become real flesh and blood. I would touch and know it with the same factual intensity with which I recognised my own body. He would come back. Just as I'd expected him to, that cold March night.

So I went to sleep, content. Very early in the morning I woke, alert, waiting. I lay still, listening intently to every tiny sound. Quiet outside, before dawn, mind drifting. Pentecost, Whit Sunday, the day of dawn, of spirit, White fire of love will burn. I must have slept. The sun was up – I jumped out of bed, suddenly feeling cold. I stood a moment in the empty hallway looking at the glass in the front door. You could always see if someone was outside on the porch. All was silent in the early Sunday morning street – never a passing car. The first time since he died I knew despair.

I stumbled on the kitchen step, went to the back door. I was tearful, torn; I couldn't sustain this, or contain myself. I began to call. I must call him, "Tom – Tom!" The calls got louder, until every vein stood out in my head and my chest heaved, the neck muscles tight like bars. The shouts were the loudest I could make, and they rebounded back from the walls, dully. I dried up, having no breath, sat down, legs all limp, in his old wooden armchair. I felt like a pile of ash after a bonfire, quite shrivelled. A cinder. A sinner.

I washed my face in cold water; dressed. It was a May morning, and we were going on a journey. The kitchen was a mess, so I worked hard. Packing the bus was good fun. It was a goodbye trip, farewell to England, so we had presents for friends, and wanted to look our best.

Rueben drove. He was learning but already very expert. I sat at the back, and still my thoughts went to the rescue, the rescuer. *Another VW bus would drive up behind us and follow. He would be driving – I must not turn round, or look to see, not try to glimpse him in the drivers mirror (that would be why I mustn't drive today). At the right moment, not to be predicted, we'd find ourselves parked together.*

An easy, early morning drive to Oxford, over the South Downs, past Harwell, Abingdon, the crown of the hill with town and domes hazy in the warmth of a soft summer morning. We planned to stop for a couple of hours. Boys could explore, go on the river maybe. Esther and I would go on our own, a wander at Esther's speed, she was four, and meet again at the bus, parked outside the Radcliffe Infirmary.

We walked slowly along. There was St Aleutias Church – the congregation coming for Whit Sunday High Mass. That was where we'd all been two years before to witness the wedding of my fiery friend and nephew and his Chinese bride ... the lotus flower. She'd worn one in her hair. The bride, the widow, the widow's mite. I pulled at my purse, all the money I could find, notes and all, and pushed the lot into the collection box on the wall by the entrance. Then we went inside. They had begun to sing. A big church with fine acoustics. The procession of choir and priests passed solemnly up the aisle.

The priests were dressed in splendid colours, rose pink and gold. A large congregation stood and sang dutifully, some diffidently; here and there someone sang with love.

I sat in a pew halfway up the aisles. Esther beside me. Some prayers, another hymn. I sat watching, reading the words. And it was as if a force came, a mighty rushing wind, an irresistible power – who was I to resist? I couldn't.

It took me, like a leaf, and whisked me on to my feet. Words came out of my mouth, echoing in vault of the church, overwhelming the hymn. I was possessed, as I'd read of in stories long ago.

Sit down! The priests and people went on singing like an army under fire. The next gust, tremendous impact. *Stop Singing!* A woman came and pulled my arm. People started to whisper and talk, the hymn went on. I was hustled into the centre aisle, Esther following.

"Be quiet!" someone said. "Behave yourself!"

I was escorted to the door – a tall man on either side. I tried to push them aside and kicked out with my sandaled feet. (Across the Atlantic, Robert Kennedy was being assassinated on this turbulent eddy of time, a tidal wave of anguish.) I shouted some more – I can't remember the words. A kindly woman had taken Esther aside. She watched but seemed uninvolved, as if it was someone else, a strange person, not her mum. I was taken into the presbytery, next to the church. It was quiet there, and a tall, burly priest came and asked me if I felt better.

I tried to explain, truthfully. "It's just like a sneeze", I said. "It comes like that, a big gasp of breath, and then those words came out. I can't stop it. I can't. It will come again, soon. I can feel it, my breath, it takes my breath away ... *aaaah God! God is love!*"

The shout echoed again, and then it was quiet in the peaceful room. Old furniture, books, a grand piano with lid down, dark polished wood in which room was reflected – as in a glass darkly ...

I remembered the picture in *Alice through the Looking Glass* where she climbs on the mantle shelf and the glass dissolves. I began telling this stranger about Tom, and about being in love, loving him, being loved, but in another time and space.

"Can you describe this? What was the thing that gave your marriage its quality?"

I began to tell him, but before I could say one word more the breath was drawn in. I felt suspended, as if it would never come out again. Again, expelling with a force using every ounce of strength, that shouted, *"Love! Love! It's bloody marvellous!"*

And by bloody I meant in the mediaeval sense, "By our lady". I knew that intellectually, although I didn't choose those words.

When I got my breath back, I told him, "I seem to be in a different space. Yesterday it was an outer space. Now I'm in inner space. I can't get back again. Like being in the reflected room you can see in the piano lid. It's a bubble. All that we see and are is happening on the outside of the bubble. But equally, all that is happening is going on in the inside of the bubble; you are either in the one or the other. I was out, and now I'm in – inner space".

The priest had a kind pink face, and he suggested it was time to go. He led me out, and we found Esther talking happily to the kind lady, who had made her a drink. Another helper joined us and walked the short distance along Woodstock Road to the Radcliffe Infirmary building.

"You'd better come in here and talk to a doctor". Esther and the lady stayed outside, and I was asked to sit in a small room and wait. Soon, a white-coated doctor came. "Tell me what's wrong".

I told him what happened in church and after.

I also told him that I was the Virgin Mary, bride of Christ, that I was Eve, the divine mother of earth and sky, a second coming, and that I didn't want to be, but that my mind kept telling me I was, and I couldn't escape.

He listened attentively and didn't contradict me. "You'd better go back home right away – go and rest, see your doctor. It will be all right".

My head felt clearer, and I went out to collect Esther. I told the lady I was OK now and took Esther's hand. We walked slowly back to the town. Inner space. Suddenly, this was not Oxford 1968 but 1938, another sequence of time. No war had occurred, my brother, Charles, was alive instead of dead in an Arakan jungle, would be at Keble College studying history. We walked round to the college, and I asked at the porter's lodge if he was in his room.

"No, not at the weekend".

I said, "We're sure to meet him in the street".

Time Out of Mind

I let Esther lead me. She tugged gently at my hand, and I followed. She trotted along gaily, quite untroubled by events of the morning, asking questions, merrily commenting on everything we saw. Yes, this was prewar Oxford, timeless, mellow.

Somehow, entranced, I found she had led me back to the infirmary. Down a side entrance used by delivery vans, past rows of bins and incinerators, iron fire escape stairways, many tall buildings. We threaded our way between the parked cars and the narrow back areas. In the last half mile or so I'd felt nervous; that was new. All through the last days, only vaguely remembered at this moment, I'd felt many things, but never nervous. This was a prickly anxiety, but wasn't about anything in particular. With this restless feeling came a curious picture – of a small room, rather like the one in which I'd met the doctor not long before. It was almost bare, and I was alone. Gradually the sensation grew that I was the room and alone within my own walls. And I would stay there, if no one remembered to come and take me out. I was aware, like a dream, that I was walking up some stone-stairs, indoors. A big building, many flights. Esther still leading me ... I would be alone in this room. I *was* alone in it. Would anyone come? The boys, the three boys; where were they? How could they find me? No one could tell them where I was. My heart began to pound; my head was spinning.

"I can't get out – oh, God, I can't get out".

I had reached the top floor. A long corridor opened out with doors along it. The boys would never find me – I *couldn't* get out. They wouldn't know where to look. I knew I was saying it out loud, then louder, then actually *screaming,* frenzied, *"I can't get out. Oh, GOD, save me. Please come and save me, please,* please!"

Esther began to cry – some people came running, voices around me. I was in a small room, some kind of office, several people with me. But I was not there – I was in the room inside my head, alone, empty.

I screamed violently: *"Jesus Christ, son of God, save me, oh Christ, Oh, God ..."* I fell on the floor. *"Help, oh help. Help me!"*

I was gasping, no breath left. On my back. My back arching up, head on the floor. "I can't, I *can't*, I can't bear it. Oh God".

I couldn't. I *would* not, no more, *–no more.* I turned over, on all fours, crawling. I began to knock my head on the hard tiled floor,

Fugue

vehement, determined. Blood poured out, down my face, blinding me. I could taste blood running into my mouth.

"Oh, God, take me away".

I couldn't lose consciousness. I was on my knees. I put my hands over my face, held them out. They were bloody. I began to wipe them on the front of my sweater. It was white, a heavy Aran knitted one ... I went on, mechanically wiping the blood off my face with my hands and smearing it over my jersey. Someone came and knelt beside me and pushed a needle deep into my thigh ... I died.

> December dark, blackness at
> Dawn – at six o'clock the morn
> Is midnight
> The promise hides, hurries not
> Slides shyly behind shadows
> The roots of spring, the seed and
> Bulb, buried in the dark,
> Wet garden, huddled in
> Earth, waiting for warmth,
> Soul-seed, germinates so
> Innocently, silent sits.
> Love is in labour
> Locked, wrestles and tears
> The seed apart, flays fragile
> Membrane
> I am dumb this day, my tongue
> Is numb with cold
> Myself the seed, the earth,
> My life is striving
> To be born. The heart splits
> Silently, spills overflowing
> The last drop, to nourish the
> New soul in its infancy
> Grow now, sweet soul
> Grieve not at growth, but see
> How the stars still glimmer

> Prick the cold dark with
> Your delicate shoot, pointing
> Skyward

I was warm. Breathing easy. A soft light on my eyelids. I wriggled my toes and fingers. There was a bandage across my head. I opened my eyes and saw a hospital ward, dim lights above the beds. It was night. A nurse came and brought me hot tea and some toast. I ate and drank gratefully. So good. Closed my eyes again, drifting, thoughts like high clouds, hazy and peaceful. Very peaceful inside … inside, outside, outer space, space somewhere, a spacey feeling, blissful and wide.

I opened my eyes again to find daylight. I could see grass and meadows outside, and a main road with big lorries and cars speeding along. I reached behind me and put on the headphones – a man's voice singing, the usual ballad, sentimental and kind. A good clear voice, very warm. I heard the words, and felt them. A new song, but the words very old, the twenty-third psalm … the valley of the shadow of death … no fear … green pastures … my cup runneth over with love, with love.

> The sun rises, I am at ease
> Morning light, golden bright
> In the East.
> Death on Friday,
> Hell on Saturday,
> Heaven on Sunday,
> Each sleep is death,
> Each waking dawn
> I rise, each day and every rising
> Raises me.
> Every day contains
> The possibility of everlasting life.
> And when I wake
> I say
> I died last night.
> And now I live again.
> My sleep was silent

Fugue

And forever,
All of myself sealed,
Completed, stilled,
And when I wake
I say
I have come back this day.
Which one is it?
Yes, Monday,
How amazing,
I actually remember
My previous incarnation
Whitsunday. Yesterday
And today and
Forever

I remembered I died, didn't I? Now, here in this place, I was in heaven. I had been to hell; yes, something happened then, an absolute absence of being me, and now I'd become aware of myself again.

It was different, another route. Perhaps ... that was it.

Death rerouting. You become aware of yourself again, wherever and whenever that could be; it might be a recognizable continuity, another connected episode; or it might be a totally brave new world, no memory, no past, present or future, but the milky warmth of swaddling clothes and a white bosom against a hungry mouth, tiny fingers closing and unfolding like daisy petals. It might be another time and place, another *space*.

Breakfast in bed, a good one, perfectly boiled egg, toast, hot tea. Amen to that. Littlebourne, a mental hospital. I got up later and looked around. I went in the chapel, part of an older building. It was empty of chairs, being redecorated. I stood by the altar and watched the sunlight on the wall. I found a chair lying in a corner and sat down in the sun, began to meditate.

Not about anything – just to sit and let the mind go inwards very gently; I'd heard that the Beatles meditated and wondered what they did. I'd learned to do it too because it sounded such a wholesome thing, to rest and enjoy some silence. A gentle, young-looking but middle-aged lady had taught me. I was given a mantra, a sound, and using this allowed the mind to dive into an area of calm and alert stillness. My mind had been diving before, but often into chaotic turmoil of restless and tormenting thoughts and fancies. Now there was a depth of peace, a background to any experience the mind (or body) could be exposed to, and when I opened my eyes after twenty minutes I was newly awake, like that morning in bed.

I felt an assurance, quite unlike anything ever before, except the sound of Tom's voice. "Jo, Jo ..."

"Yes, Tom".

I would hear that sound in my head along with my mantra drifting into the joy of this silence.

I walked back into the hospital. I was told I should see the doctor, so I waited to be called. A woman sat near, moaning, quietly, repeating over and over again "I can't get out, *I can't get out*".

My turn came and I went in. It was a comfortable airy room. He encouraged me to talk, and I told him what I could. I wanted to tell him everything, but there wouldn't be time. I tried to explain to myself as well as to him about being Mary, as well as Jo. How being in love with someone who was dead was not just a mind feeling but a body fact. How I'd wanted to die too, to get the two halves together, to mend the split heart. That somehow the whole thing had taken off into a kind of archetypal situation, Mary the bridge to join the pieces; the bride and groom, Jesus, a sort of Trinity, father, best man and groom: Tom.

He heard me out, didn't denounce me or laugh at me. I felt just for a moment a flash, that he was there to represent Tom, a delegate to speak for him. I was given confidence and felt good, ordinary again.

The next morning I was sent to Nuffield Hospital for a head X-ray and encephalograph reading. There was a big lump on my head, but it didn't ache. I was immensely interested in these elaborate mechanisms and wanted to ask about them, but no one had much time to explain. While I waited I thought about the kids. The boys had gone back to the VW van and found Esther. She had been able to tell the people with me where to find the van – it was parked just outside. They hadn't waited there long when the boys came. They all returned to the building where I'd been given the injection. It was the maternity department of the

Radcliffe. Top floor. My screams had upset the women in the labour ward. They thought it was someone having a baby.

Rueben had rung the mental hospital and heard that I was unconscious and would be for many more hours, about fifteen, as I'd had a massive dose of the anticonvulsant medication paraldehyde.

My thigh hurt for a week; the doctor with his needle was the answer to my pleas – he had saved me from hell; as far as I could tell in that time and place he was God, or for that matter Tom or Rueben, an advocate or mediator …

Rueben took his brothers and Esther back home to wait for my discharge.

"Mrs Harding, come with me, we're going to make an encephalograph test on that head of yours".

They sat me in a special chair. Beside me was a panel with dials and a lighted screen, a delicate green with a hovering line of white on it. A lot of wires were affixed to my scalp and I was told to sit still and quietly.

I said, "I'll meditate so I won't be nervous and my mind will be quiet – OK?"

"Fine, do what you like".

I shut my eyes and the mantra came; I found myself, as often, aware on two levels; a consciousness of the outside; the movements, sounds, voices coming through as if from a distance, hearing but not thinking. And this was supported and held poised by the stillness within me, a sort of corridor between polarities.

I hear them say, "It isn't working. That's funny, it did last time we used it".

"Well, there's no reading there; nothing's happening".

I opened my eyes.

"We don't seem to be getting anything out of this machine. Wait a minute, and we'll put it on someone else; see what happens then".

One of the technicians sat down and was wired up. Machine on. Plenty of activity on the screen this time.

"Ah, that's more like it. Well, it's working then".

"All right, lady, back you go".

"OK. Can I meditate this time too?"

"Sure, you may as well; makes no difference; you can do what you like with your own mind".

I closed my eyes while they adjusted the equipment again. Silence. I felt myself going deep, very easy and peaceful.

"All right, we'll just have to accept the reading – it's virtually a straight line. I dunno? Perhaps you've just a normal brain! Well, we tried it on the other bloke, and we know it's in order – best we can do".

The X-ray department were very brusque with me, looking for skull damage maybe. But possibly for a tumour. Anyway, no one ever let on. I gathered it was all OK. An ambulance ride back to the other hospital – two more days resting there. I was not given any drugs. I felt quite easy; my head did not hurt at all.

I often heard the woman crying softly still, in a monotonous, dry tone: "I can't get out; I can't get out".

It made me ache to hear it. I didn't know of anything I could do, but I wanted to help. Someday, I would know how and I'd let her out, or someone like her.

I was waiting happily in the hospital entrance. The VW rolled round the gateway and out jumped George, Tom's friend and mine; he looked the part, like a father, as the boys and Esther gathered round. George, an art historian, broad shouldered, bald headed, had a rosy complexion like an English apple, and the manner of a rural bishop, a cheerful and benign man. He greeted us with his usual warmth, quite unabashed by my evident aberrations. There were friendly hugs and grins all round. A family reunion.

We drove back home, and I felt refreshed and in good order. I thought I'd got through some kind of barrier, another layer peeled off, and the new growth exposed was surviving, even if fragile.

So we set out on our journey again. This time we drove through Oxford, and on to Rutland, so that Esther could see the house where she was born. It was a June day filled with white clouds, the May blossoms in full petals in the quiet green meadows. White lambs and slow rivers (*in pastures green he leadeth me ...*). We stayed the night in Whissendine in an old cottage, washed white walls, wooden beams, and roses up the wall.

I went to bed, shared it with Esther. I lay quite still so I would not wake her. She was already asleep, her long curly hair like a cloud across the pillow. I went to sleep too, but woke at about one a.m. Something was happening in my mind again; a dream? No, it wasn't a dream. I was wide awake. But my eyes were shut and this sensation persisted. A movement, like a film being run at great speed, a fast rewind on a tape recorder. Images and sounds flashed past at a great speed. I felt weightless, and my limbs were numb. It was like being sucked into a vortex, spinning faster and faster, the apex of that tunnel receding in front of me.

In the beginning, in the beginning, it is the word. Back to the beginning, and all time will cease. Time is flowing, it is reaching a climax, an apex. Time is over (did it ever begin?). "Behold I have made all things new ..." Infinity, infinity, plunging into infinity, infinite speed, infinite stillness, a moment that has no beginning, no end ...

I opened my eyes. The light came in, soft, scarcely perceptible. It was daylight, before sunrise. I felt dizzy and shut my eyes again. Later, it didn't matter when, I got up. Esther's sleeping face was like a pale pink rose, a dawn sky. I tiptoed to the window and pushed it outwards, wide, put my head out. I was awestruck. This was a new time, a new creation. The old one had dissolved; I was a sort of Eve, and this was the first day.

Below the window the roses climbed the walls of the stone cottage. Cotswold stones, rough hewn, many hues of ochre, brown, and a warm pink-purple where the iron had tinted it. The roses were red and one was in full bud just at the windowsill.

A light rain had fallen, and the flower was covered with brilliant water drops, hanging along the edge of each unfolding petal and outlining the leaves. The rose held my eye, and I was dissolved into it, became it, as the singer becomes the pure sound, and I hung, like the silver water-drops, reflecting every detail, the hanging sky, the grass below, the houses in the still dreaming village. The silence had a quality never before perceived, by me, at least. I was silence, the grass, the rain. I crept back to bed beside Esther.

"All right", I said to myself. "Where do we go from here?"

"Just where you go – it does itself, nature does it, 'you' do it, 'we do it. Who is we? All things work together ..." Thus the answer, emerging from a deeper realm of my own consciousness

My soul sits still, this
Is my dawn.
Blushing I sit, pierced through the
Brow; the archer with his
Bow, bent to the stretch of
Time, centred the target
Of my mind, and slew
My self, one dazzling
Dart (or many, none can tell)
The mark to make, or mar
Hung time around my
Shoulders like a cloak,
The Milky Way a veil of
Light, embroidered with
Fickle, prickling stars, covers
My head. My breast, my
Face, is bare – pierce me,
Thread through the weft,
Weaving your robe,
Wear me, hand woven out of
Thrums, and I will wrap you
Gather your grief in my arms
Love; come love,
Come.

From Rutland, then the smallest County in England, to Cambridgeshire, driving through the flat fen country, the water meadows and the husky pollarded willow trees, brilliant greens and silver greys, the corn rising in the fields. We kept losing the way going cross-country. Had the usual good humoured but passionate arguments about where we were. For a homecoming, my native land. My friend's house was a manor, a mellow ancient home standing in one of the most beautiful gardens imaginable. A warm welcome and an excellent meal. Everything was easy – the friendship, and a perfection of domesticity. But this was the home where Tom and I had spent our last weekend together. I would sleep in that same bed, and I knew I would not get away with it. Some residue of anguish was yet inside and would come to the surface. I couldn't guess how. I didn't anticipate. I knew I would have to experience it.

Once again I felt that prickling tension. I visited some friends in nearby villages, had a good talk, and explained something of our life these past two years. A day and night passed and the feeling grew. I had to enact something; I did not want to, but I could not choose my role; it was something to do with Abraham and Isaac. An ancient, irrevocable sacrifice, a curious anger at myself for instigating it and then, gradually, this anger taking form (but all the time it was a play, a bit of acting. The frightening thing was that I *had* to play it).

I woke in the morning in that bright room and helped Esther dress. Her hair was long, thick and magnificently curly, a light brown, finely textured. Very beautiful. I brushed it out and, as usual, she yelped when I reached a tangle. I grabbed a pair of scissors which seemed almost to have materialised on the table, took my daughter by the hair, grasping all of it in one hand, and pulled her across the room. She screamed and jerked away. Then I cut off her hair. It fell on the floor in a heap of curls. I was breathless and crying

"Oh, Esther, it always made you cry! Every time I brushed it out. I cannot bear it".

I put an equal amount of hair inside each of her bedroom slippers.

"Now you'll have fur-lined slippers – that will be better than having it on your head".

She'd stopped crying, as she wasn't hurting. This intrigued her. She said, "Oh, that's nice, I like that. Furry lined slippers – let's put them on. Yes, they fit better".

She said no more but hurried off to the other children.

Later that day Joseph came upstairs to that room. I looked at him, my son, a twin, and saw his great strength and self-possession, 14 years of it. Inwardly I blessed him. Outwardly (everything got back to front this day) I took him by the arm and pulled him to the open window. I picked up the scissors and held them, pointing at him. "I'm going to throw you out".

I walked him forward and pressed him on to the windowsill. He was facing me. He did not look scared.

"I mean it", I said.

He saw that I did. I pushed harder, and he began to resist me. He simply reached over and took the scissors out of my hand, held my wrists, and made me sit on the bed. I was weak in comparison with his strength. He was not a child. I fled out into the passage and came to the stairs, where I began to scream. Very loudly and determinedly.

Rueben came running up the stairs. I was swearing – shrieking and swearing *Jesus bloody Christ*. I hit up across his face with all my strength. He was a tall lad of 16, very strong and broad shouldered. Tears came into his eyes for a moment. I do not remember that he said anything to me. I went downstairs and got in the bus. I drove it out and went down the main road. I drove at great speed, faster than I had ever done and recklessly, crossing traffic lights and halt signs without slowing up. I drove as if blind.

Then I began to dream about my other twin son, Jonas. The dream was that every danger I perpetrated on the road had endangered *him,* and by now I had already placed him in great peril. I must return at once. I must get there in time; I could save him. But if I drove fast and did not obey the rules of safety, I would imperil him even more. And then I might be too late. I did not know what this danger might be. I knew I must not hurry, that there was a delicate balance of time involved. I was trembling all over, hands sweating and heart thumping painfully, a harsh fluttering of excitement in my stomach. "O Absalom, my son, my son".

I turned off the main road, into the winding country lanes where I could only go at twelve to twenty mph. My mouth was dry, breath coming in jerks. I turned the bus in through the narrow gate on to the gravel drive and jumped out. Ran round the side of the house to the lawn where I could hear children playing and laughing. Esther was playing croquet with the girls. No sign of the boys. I asked her.

"In the barn, I expect".

I had a picture in my head of a body swinging heavily from a rope. I ran through the gate in the wall to the other yard, the barn door open wide, dark shadows within. I stopped. I didn't want to see. A movement caught my eye – I took a couple of steps forward. Jonas, swinging, not from a rope, but on it, feet firmly tucked around a big knot, arms over the head, gracefully swinging and turning, spiralling round and round,

Fugue

the shafts of sunlight in the huge tithe barn falling in blithe patches on the floor.

"Hullo, OK?"

"Yes, fine".

I went outside. It seemed the task (what task?) was over. Or not quite. There was me. I hadn't done *me* (what *doing* was this anyway?).

"There is no remission of sins without shedding of blood".

"You must be joking!"

>Someone had the idea of a play-planet,
>A happy hunting ground amusement park –
>Go there and enjoy yourself
>It's all wish fulfilment there, you wish,
>You think, your think comes true
>Instantly.
>The friend you have not met for fifteen years
>For you to love,
>The enemy you never fought for you to
>Fight and win
>Or lose, the wild tiger that you conjured up
>Perhaps a fairy tale or two,
>Alice and the Duchess, Peter Rabbit,
>Gandalf, and Robin Hood,
>All being truly themselves for your adventure.
>We wish what we are our thoughts,
>Our nature too.
>What we most wish for often
>We most fear.
>I think the world is such a game
>No one ever told us how to play.
>Or if they did we forgot or ignored the rules
>A game without any isn't fun
>Is that why we often hate playing this one?
>Or did they change the rules half way through
>Without telling anyone
>Just to make it more exciting?

A little girl of 7 went to bed at five.
She took a candle with her to see by.
She had no light plug in her room.
Always made her bed by candlelight –
Where did she lead that little flame
And what game was she playing in her mind?
The little flame reached out and touched her dress,
Longed to embrace her, take her in its arms.
The little flame grew like an opening flower
Second by second, reaching, enfolding,
Transforming, consuming, living its own nature.
The child's screams are choked with smoke;
Her tiny brother runs into the kitchen.
"She's on fire, she's on fire!"
Suddenly everyone runs, screams, cries, gasps.
(What were they all thinking and talking of at just that moment?)
Her uncle throws a heavy blanket round the torch,
Snatches the burnt offering from the altar
Just in time.
Who put her there? I wonder.

After supper, the family in bed, I went into the children's playroom. All in darkness. The new puppy was there, a playful, cheerful terrier, a little aggressive but friendly enough. I picked him up and took him in to the kids' lavatory and locked the door. I stroked him and talked to him for a minute or two, and then I sat down and peed. I took off my pants and sat on the floor, back to the wall with my knees against my chest. The puppy came up, and I let him nose his way up to my body. He began to growl gently and opened his mouth, showing sharp white teeth. He smelt the animal, sweating odour of me, exposed like that, and vigorously explored me with his nose, sniffing and growling, and then he began to tear at me with his small teeth. I could bear it at first, but soon I began to cry out. I could have stopped him quite easily, but somehow I knew I must not; I knew I had to let him do what he wanted and experience this masochistic fulfilment. I cried out several times as he bit into my most tender flesh, and knowingly, that I was in a reverse of all reason and order, I put it in to words, *"Oh dog, oh dog, oh my dog"*.

Someone rattled the door. My friend's voice. "Are you all right?" Anxious, strained.

"Don't worry. I'm just coming". I got to my feet. Waited a moment to hear her feet receding into the distance. Then I opened the door, left the dog where he was, and stumbled in the dark up the back stairs. I got into bed. I was very sore. My host came. He handed me a couple of pills.

"Take these", he said. "My wife's gone to bed. She can't take anymore".

"I don't blame her", I said.

"Neither could I".

I swallowed the pills and fell asleep almost immediately.

We left in the morning. My friends, good friends. I loved them. They looked pale and upset. I was sad to leave them this way. Maybe it would be years before we met again. Going to America I felt I had used them, abused their hospitality. But it was done, and I had to say goodbye.

I had a lot to think about on the way home. One thing was for sure. Whatever was happening, it was different in one respect. Since that awakening, the deepest, most compulsive experience was always accompanied by a new clear consciousness of that experience. I could not avoid these happenings – in a way, I felt I didn't instigate them – they happened *to* me. But instead of a sense of being lost, hopelessly invaded, and split by activities of my mind which were so frighteningly unfamiliar, for most of the time I had a curious sense of déjà vu. I felt a bit like a puppet being skilfully played, but I myself, or a part of me, was pulling the strings. It seemed to me, as we drove south past the green corn and the hayfields growing high (would I miss England too much?) that I somehow had to get through a number of life experiences, without which my understanding of them would be superficial; empathy perhaps, but not a concrete reality. Now, I would see not darkly but face to face.

I felt some respite, but I knew for sure that there was more to come. I did not feel this as anxiety but more as an intense curiosity, like an explorer might feel when he discovers an old map, or reaches the limits of known territory. This was indeed a major exploration. I felt sure that this territory had been opened up before, but had anyone returned to tell the tale or map the routes? I hoped, if I could make it, that I would meet someone else someday, who would describe a similar journey, a travelling companion. If I had to be mad, and I knew I was, it had better be useful some way. Like the fact of Tom. His death could not be destructive to us living ones. His still-living influence would bring us to life as we had never been before.

Ransom was the old word for it. If I could not stop what was going on in my mind I could cooperate with it (*it* must be me too) and help a process which was quite surely intent on its route. (I remembered Jung had said we should make friends with our own unconscious.)

Back at home things looked benevolent in the June sun. The garden had grown. It wasn't really a garden, more a yard, but it was a riot of leafy green, and flowers were out, one pink rose especially, about six inches across.

I went to see the doctor and told him a little about myself, and asked him to give me a week off from work. I didn't feel I could get in front of a class of kids, teaching. It was enough to face myself.

I felt relaxed and cheerful, though I had to cope with some new and disturbing thoughts. I went into the garden after the boys had gone off to school and lay on a rug in the sun. It was hot. I hung sheets on the line to dry, and they made a tent-like screen. I took off my clothes, careful to see that I would not be spied on by neighbours. It was immensely relaxing, blissful. I needed that. My mind was tattered and torn like the bit of my body that got bitten. My own doing. Yes, but ... oh well; the sun's rays made gorgeous pulsating colours on my closed lids. I slept. I bought Esther a bride dolly, and some dark glasses for me. Two days I lived in the garden. It was a heat wave. The boys came in and out, happily engaged in their usual doings. I felt the healing warmth of the sun and was more aroused by my unpredictable love than ever.

This took me on a new theme – of rebirth, renewal. I dreamed that my body would regenerate itself, make new out of the old. Cell by cell.

I was convinced that somehow the expression of love could give birth to itself – parthenogenesis. Love must recreate itself in the nature of things. I wanted a manifestation of the fact that I felt reborn.

Fugue

Now when ray eyes are filled with
Sleep
Take off my clothes and let me
Weep
There's none to share,
or care or
Mend
But one, who comes, his love to
Send.
Be not amazed, you little
Flock
The night is past, the rending
Shock
None can defy, nor deign to
Hold
The tide will flow, for love is
Bold.
We wait for life, we ask not
Why
The flux is fixed, we cannot
Sigh
Endeavour all, the night is
Spent
Make love, make life, the veil is
Rent
The trumpet sounds, the dead
Awake
Mankind will live, for all loves'
Sake
Come take my hand where friendship is
And dance with me the way to bliss

I felt happy without my clothes in the warm garden. By the end of the week I felt sure I would be easier, thoughts would settle, a new order would emerge. I knew I had been having a nervous breakdown but did not think myself as sick, or needing treatment. Just some time.

The doctor came one afternoon when I was naked in the garden. One of the boys came out and said he was in the house.

I replied, "Bring him out here. He's quite used to human bodies. He won't mind me be being without my clothes. That's his job".

"OK", Rueben said. "I'll fetch him out".

He came through the back door, and I could tell at once that he did not approve of me! He spoke brusquely and prescribed tablets. Then he said he would come again tomorrow and bring another doctor to see me. I told him about my experience in Oxford, the reason for my wounded head, the results of X-ray and EEGs, about the help meditation had been to me. I had the feeling that he disregarded everything I said to him, somehow not understanding any of it, and I felt oddly uneasy.

The doctors came next day. I talked some more, innocently explaining some of my feelings and impressions, my sexual excitement, which had no object, except that it was there. They started telling me that I needed to accept treatment as a voluntary patient. Not in the main hospital – there were nice villas in the grounds, very comfortable. No loss of freedom – it would be a time of further rest. A sharp stab of fear hit me for a second. Then the persuasive, reassuring voices penetrated the flashback thoughts I was having.

"All right", I was saying. "I suppose it's the best thing".

I didn't feel at all happy. But I did not resist. No, I needed to go and see what would happen.

The boys and I talked together. They said they could manage on their own. Georgecould sign up as foster parent and keep an eye on things while I was away. They insisted they would be OK and preferred it that way. Independence all round; I went off quite blithely, feeling that all would be well, and said goodbye to everyone as if I were going on a holiday.

When I arrived, I was shown a nice bright room in a spacious house. About six beds there, a dayroom on the ground floor with a TV, a kitchen with access to tea and coffee, and a place to wash clothes. I felt rather happy, even a little elated. It could even be fun. I began to talk to the others, as usual, rather a lively chatterer. The garden outside looked inviting, and it was all very far away from the other ward I'd occupied before. Nurses were easy and would stop for talks.

Fugue

The first day I explored, found a country lane at the back, ploughed fields beyond. It was really rather pleasant, peaceful even.

I slept well that first night and looked forward to the next day. I was summoned to the doctor's office. To my horror I was told I was to be given drugs. I was deeply appalled, remembering the reaction I'd had last time.

"No, please, not more drugs".

"It would be so much better just to take this time to rest and recover".

"Not pills!"

"You have to accept this, Mrs Thomas. They are necessary".

"Isn't there anything else? Can't you make an exception? Please!"

"Well, you could have an injection instead of pills".

"All right, I'll try it that way; it may not have the same bad effect".

So I submitted. It felt like a prison sentence. The first two days were not too bad. I felt and was active. I did some yoga asanas in the garden, climbed a few trees (this was ordinary activity for me at home), explored the woods and fields at the back. About the third day it all began to go wrong. I began to feel a pressure in the head – a sort of clinging disorientation, an enervating lethargy at times, and a sense of oppression. I couldn't tell what was me myself and what was the result of the injections.

I learned from home that my aunt had come to look after the family. She visited me and seemed very nervous and remote from me – disapproving perhaps.

I began to feel more and more invalidated, and when I saw the doctors again I begged them to stop the injections. They insisted I continue. The dizziness persisted, and I began to be afraid. I cheered myself up by running in the garden. I meditated. The patients in this villa usually went home at weekends. I discovered that I was not to be allowed to visit my home, or the children. A patient had to be signed out by someone at home. My aunt declared herself unable to take that responsibility. I felt isolated, homeless. The whole scene suddenly became menacing. My family had unaccountably rejected me. I felt like a whipped child, no one to turn to. I wanted very badly to go home. It was a compulsion.

Next day, a Sunday, I went over to the chapel. A Roman Catholic service was in progress. I sat down in a pew at the back. A handful of patients were scattered around the spacious interior. The priest walked slowly up the aisle from behind me. I could not see his face until he turned at the altar steps. I gasped and watched him. I was amazed and aghast. This man was Tom's double, so like him – his walk, his gestures, the angle of his head – I could have wept.

I said to myself, "Jo, it's just imagination, wishful thinking, you want to resurrect him anyway".

But my eyes were telling me, not my heart. I had to accept what I could see. And of all people, a Catholic priest, no doubt a celibate, dedicated man with a job to do. Oh God, what a trick to play on me.

I went back to the villa after the service, my mind in turmoil. It was more than two years now since Tom died and the sight of this man tore open the scar of grief. I was feeling heavy and light-headed all at once. Those injections played hell with me. It was time for my next one. I couldn't bear it.

I went upstairs and shouted, "Please leave me alone; why don't you treat me like a human being?"

I let out in a frenzy of sound, all my fear and loneliness. I was desperately asking for help, for communication. A male nurse came and steered me towards my bed.

"Look", he said, "that's not fair on the other patients. They don't want to hear you doing that – put your head into the pillow, pull the quilt over your head, and then you can scream all you want".

It sounded like good sense. And I did as he said – I plunged my face into the pillow and screamed and shouted until I was exhausted and had no voice left at all. For several days after, I could only croak out a whisper.

I wanted to go home. I wanted to be with the kids; it became a necessity. I decided to discharge myself. I knew vaguely that I could do that. I was a voluntary patient – I would have the right. I talked to a nurse and wrote out on a piece of paper that I was signing myself out. I went upstairs and packed my case, carried it downstairs and out to the drive. The nurse signed my paper for me and said she would need to get someone else inside to sign it. I waited. In a few minutes she came out with another older nurse. They both walked alongside me down the path. One of them offered to carry my case.

Fugue

Halfway, as we neared the main building, the senior nurse stopped us. "We have to go into the other building first", she said. "There's someone else we have to see before you leave".

I felt very uncomfortable walking towards that main hospital block. In fact, I began to be afraid as we approached the main entrance. But we passed that, the nurse with my case leading. She went straight up to a side door, took out a key, opened it, and we went in. She immediately locked it after us. To my complete amazement I found myself in the outer corridor of the women's ward I had been in two years before.

> I am hungry and thirsty.
> My tears have used up all the water.
> (The tap has been dripping for years –
> When will the plumber come?)
> I wake early and the thoughts leap
> Through a loop
> Out on the dim circumference of time.
> I tread a tightrope
> One step at a time never stopping.
> You, on the other side of the
> Circle coming towards me
> Seeking my centre, not yet in flesh
> Finding yourself a form
> Fecund, factual, free.
> Oh, fear not to be free,
> My Lord, you abusing and abused.
> Used are we all, absurdly
> In the dharma of love
> Cannot you see
> There is no abuse if I love you
> Even forgiveness is given away
> No blame or chain or claim
> But arms, thighs, eyes open wide
> To receive you, sweet Lord.

"We feel you are not fit enough to return home. Your family aren't ready to have you back. You'll remain here for further tests and observation".

I was ushered to the main, only-too-familiar ward. I felt numb, unbelieving. It couldn't be true. I was a voluntary patient. What had gone wrong? I had been upset, yes, but I did no harm to anyone. I had only wanted to be home again. The pain of this betrayal (what else could you call it?) was just one more.

I got into the bed. The only available one was stuck out in the middle of the ward between the other beds, right up against the wash basins. I felt exposed and huddled under the sheets. I was totally deflated. I had done all my screaming, like the Red Queen in *Alice*, before the event. The very same nurse who had held my hand when I was so split before was on night duty. At least one person here was familiar and kind. The others were probably kind too, but I did not know their faces yet.

The following day was grim, and I complained bitterly about how I'd been conned into the locked ward, and this roused everyone, patients and staff alike, to an equally negative response to me. I got no sympathy, This was evidently no way to go on. I felt caged in, and the feeling grew all day. By nightfall I was in the grip of acute claustrophobia. I really wanted to get out. I remembered my plans and frustrations of two years ago, the girl and the plate glass. I went to bed and lay awake.

The night seemed endless. If I could go home I could talk to my aunt; she loved me and would understand. I would get through to her, overcome her fears, and get back the easy communication of times past. Everything would be OK. A warm welcome, a cup of tea, talk it all over. If I got up quietly I could get out somehow, but a great weight seemed to press down on me from all the dimensions of this big room. I must, *I must, now*.

I got out of bed, barefoot; it was quieter that way. Slipped my blue silk caftan – it was made from a sari given me by my aunt – over my head; I had to pass the curtained cubicle where the night nurse sat. She had her back to me. I went to an alcove in the corner where tall windows looked out onto a small lawn with a high privet hedge and fence around it. I paused for a second and took in the sleeping people on the beds nearby, the dim light at the far end where the nurse was reading. Picked up a chair, and raised it above my head, brought it down as hard as I could against the glass. The noise was deafening, and I was covered with broken glass. The tension broke inside me, and I clambered out on to the glass-strewn windowsill. I was fast, and faster when I heard all kinds of noises behind me. There was quite a drop to the ground below but plenty of glass down there too.

I jumped and then ran across the grass, plunged into the hedge, and somehow found a huge amount of energy to lift myself up over the fencing. Another long jump down and then across the wide lawns and tree-lined paths between the hospital and the road. It was raining softly, very mild and quiet, the air indescribably sweet to breathe. I was euphoric, in a state of joy. I was free.

I ran easily and wasn't out of breath. I got to the main entrance, which was open ... I stood a moment in a laurel thicket from which I could see the road. I knew if I crossed it there was an alley behind the houses alongside a recreation ground. A quiet lane led from there in the direction of the road I had to take. There was not a soul in sight. I felt roughness of tarmac under my feet. Then pavement. Then the earthy tread of the alley path. Here in the lamplight I could see I was covered with blood. My hands were badly cut across the palms, and my right knee had a huge curious gash. I walked fast now and out across the big road, going to the sea front. I chose a route of side streets. All the lights were orange ones. No one who saw me would know I was bloody. The colour was changed to a dull brown by the orange lights.

I kept walking. It took about half an hour. I met no one. I went to the back gate, hidden in a tiny alley. Another climb, and into the back yard. Back door open, thank God. (What did I *expect,* coming in at three a.m. in that state?)

I turned on the light in the kitchen. What a joy to be here; but I must not waste time. I wiped my face and hands, but they were still a mess, and then I went to my room where my aunt was sleeping and called her softly. She woke, and I turned on the light.

"I have come to talk to you. I need to talk".

She was obviously very frightened. I had no idea I would appear so alien to her. She got out of bed very quickly and went straight to the phone, rang the police and then the hospital. She was deeply upset and very angry. I could see there would be no talking then.

As the police station was next door, they were not long in arriving. I was by now aware of the pain of my gashes. I agreed to come with them after I'd had some tea. I made it and gave them all some. There were four or five of them; I think they thought I could be dangerous. I talked and joked with them and then the ambulance came.

I think my aunt needed treatment for shock as much as I did. She had nothing to say to me, which was a small wonder. They put sixteen stitches in at the hospital and then placed me in a different ward upstairs, where there was no jumping out of the window. (With the hindsight of six years passed I am painfully aware that in releasing my own stress I created as much, perhaps for my loved ones to carry – possibly by now they have forgiven me.)

I was in a side ward, bare and very small. My stitches hurt, and I began to think about the building I was in. This was the upper floor. The ward where I had broken the window was on the ground floor. I noticed an entrance door in the same building below ground level. It was reached by a flight of steps. It dawned on me that there was a huge ward, unseen, windowless, a series of tunnels opening out into narrow spaces. It was very hot, airless. If you were a 'bad' type of patient you were taken there, and maybe it would be many months, possibly years before you were brought back. People would forget about you, go on living without you, adjusting themselves to life as if you had never existed, or else resigning themselves to another route, missing you but managing without you … If Tom had been in such a place, unknown to me, my life would not be changed any more than it has now, in this box-like place (I had been there before, hadn't I, in my mind?). I was a 'bad' patient now; I had broken the rules and a window. I was an outcast. I felt rebellious and angry. I was not sure if I really believed in this subterranean punishment block, but it was in my mind, like the memory of a nightmare, for a long time.

When I was told the next morning that I was "Under section, four weeks". This is a Court order to prevent a vulnerable patient from leaving the hospital. I felt the caged feeling come back more strongly than ever. Except that now there was nowhere to go, I wanted to escape – it was an obsession. I made up a scenario in my head. There would be a plan, not made with words but by thought transference. A rendezvous would take place. The kids would take the VW bus with all necessities for a long journey. I'd get out of this locked place somehow and walk out of the town. The bus would pass me on the road, and it had to slow up for traffic lights, I saw myself running, and the door would be open wide. Warm hands would pull me in, and we would all be on our way, laughing.

I dimly saw another episode: a night journey, dawn breaking and the outline of mountains in the distance – Wales. At a country crossroads, slowing down to watch the sun rise and brew some tea. We would stop then, and a man on the grass was waiting. He comes over to join us. No one says a word, but quietly the jobs are done. Kettle filled, gas lit, mugs set out. Esther moves over, and without comment or care sits innocently beside him. He puts his arm around her and she snuggles close. I pour tea, and we all smile. "That's great – smashing cuppa tea". I turn at last, daring to look at him. "Hullo, Tom". No drama, no amazement. A great warmth and delight in the heart. We just go on from there – no time, only this present moment, no other. "All right then, fellers – let's be on the move. Shall I drive?"

> We wake at six
> Or half-past, maybe
> Half awake, talking
> In hushed voices, as in
> A church or in a library
> Or in the presence of
> The dying
> This is the time for the first
> Cup of tea and also
> For truth
> Truth comes easily in
> The first moments of waking
> When sad dreams
> Are banished by the
> Coming day.

It's hard to cry oneself
Awake,
Though many sad folk
Have cried themselves
To sleep, or dream
A fill of fear.
At this time we know
Ourselves, all of our
Selves at one
Quietly, without stress
Or tangles
For a man and a woman
This is the time for
The excellence of tenderness
Joy
Tempered by sleep

Several days passed. I was moved back into the women's ward downstairs again. One morning I noticed a small pane of glass missing in the conservatory window. It was raining, a fine misty rain, not cold. No one was in sight as everyone was getting their elevenses. I put my head through, then shoulders – I could just make it. I wriggled until my hands were down to the floor on the outside and then pulled my legs through. I crouched for a moment, out of sight from the inside, and then crept round the edge of the small lawn very slowly until I reached the shrubs at the side. This was away from the dayroom, only overlooked by unoccupied bed wards. I climbed the now familiar fence and walked quite slowly over to the park ground beyond. A young man about 19 years old was sitting on a bench in the rain. I sat down too.

"Would you like to come on a journey with me, away from here?"
"OK".

I was wearing that white Aran sweater. He had on a plain blue one.
"Change sweaters with me, so we won't be identified so easily".

He pulled his off, and we swapped. Then we walked out to the main road and down towards Franken. We passed a taxi office. I found a taxi, and we asked the man to take us to Winchester. I had an address of a friend there. I paid the three pound fare by cheque. The driver was a bit astonished but accepted it.

> I am on fire
> Fire-full with the folly of love
> Riding an ass
> A fool to do what I do
> And go where I go
> (All things must pass)
> Out beyond time
> In behind mind, over space
> Balming the torn
> Our souls will blend
> Calming the anger and blame
> Making amend
> Shunning no passable path
> Sharing the load
> (An easy yolk)
> Riding together,
> Gathering hope as we go
> The merry folk
> Never fear little flock
> Though we may be.
> Kingdom in sight
> Hour before dawn the darkest
> As everyone knows
> Sunrise within, the rim
> (Steadily grows bright)

My friend Ellen was in, and her boyfriend, Peter, too. They welcomed me. I felt at home, easy, for the first time since I'd left my own house. I told them truthfully about my escape. Someone in the hospital had told me that if I could stay out for three days, I could not be made to go back. I wanted to stay with them for three days.

These two treated me as if I were a normal human being. Did not question me, or ask me to leave. I talked to them. They listened; they were the first people to do this for a long time, and I felt quite different, whole, while I was with them. It was an immense relief. I stayed two nights. The third I could not sleep. I felt hunted again and recognised that a hunted person is no freer than a person locked in.

I got on a train and went back to the house. I went up the back stairs and talked to my student lodgers. They told the boys, who came into their room to see me. We all talked together, a proper family conference, and I felt supported, validated. I felt like taking advice. The arrogance and rebelliousness melted, transformed by friendship. I agreed with myself and with them to go back to the hospital, 'do my time', and then accept whatever was suggested thereafter. I rang for an ambulance and admitted myself back into the ward.

I found a piece of wood in the yard of the occupational therapy centre; elm, with a Y fork in it. A log cut from an old tree. It was well seasoned. I took it to the carpentry shop, and the instructor gave me a bench and let me use the tools. They were not really carving tools, but they would suffice. The man in the workshop was friendly and helpful. They also left me to get on with my own affairs. I started to work and gradually became so absorbed in it that I did not want any other activity. I had come through. No sooner than I had this clarity and calm within when the shattering news came that I was to have a further course of ECTs.

Just as before, my comment was, "But I feel better. It's OK now – all I need is time".

Why *now*? I had to submit; the month of confinement passed. The ECTs were like the first ones, but more readily accepted. I resigned myself to them. Then my aunt left, and my kids invited me home with John's authority. Or at least, John invited me for the weekends, and I went home in part. We began to be a family again. My visa from America came through, and we prepared for Exodus. I wanted a new world, a new life, to leave sorrow behind.

Ithaca in New York state sounded like paradise. A few weeks before we were due to leave, we learned it was to be Chicago instead. It didn't sound too much like paradise, but we all wanted to go anyway.

(Before I left the hospital, I asked to be shown the basement. The assistant matron did this herself. We went down amount the labyrinth of pipes and conduits, passed boilers and coke piles. Hot and airless, yes ... you could make a nice thriller for the telly with a setting like that.)

Chicago was not madness, but it was difficult. We only stayed eleven months and returned to South Wales. Life had a mellower atmosphere. I found a roomy Victorian semidetached in a pleasant tree-lined street. We all worked hard to make a home. I felt content and welcome in this place. The first year was happy and calm. I worked in the house and garden. The following summer I took a job teaching, for one term, in a comprehensive school. A week before the end of term a boy asked me why I was leaving. I explained that my job there was temporary.

He replied with intended insult, "Thought you was going to Whitfield!"

He was referring to the local 'bin'. He grinned. I was thrown, caught. I hit him. The class was stunned. So was I. I told them as well as I could that you don't make a joke about mental hospitals, or despise the people who need them. I soon forgot this scene, preparing to go on holiday to Ireland. Our last holiday as a family together, plus Rueben's girlfriend. It was everything one could have hoped for. The end of an epoch. After this it would be me and Esther: I'd be without my menfolk. I landed a good job for the September term, teaching in a country comprehensive school.

> I shall write my lines now as the pen
> Puts down in just this way whatever comes;
> Love must win and want to know the whole,
> Hate is a fallacy and cheats the soul.
> The April rain falls on the white pear trees,
> Silence is here, peace within peace for the taking,
> Life is abundant, living has no severity
> Put out your hands to the soft rain on waking.
> Self speaks to self in the stillness of mind
> Words come like rain in the spring,
> Softer than ear can catch, kinder than kinship,
> Such are the deep intuitions of friendship.

After Ireland I went to a residential course for ten days to do some more meditation. It was conducted by a Hindu monk, Swami

Satyananda, a supremely intelligent and enlightened man who taught us a great deal. All this spring and summer I'd been 'visited' by that disembodied love-ness, a counterpart of the IS-ness described by the Buddhists. I'd got used to it in a way and didn't so much look for an embodiment of this fact. I nearly always found that if I focused my attention from it to a person, that the sensation faded. It was not for me to manipulate in any way, and I had no voluntary control over it. But I did notice that it occurred in contexts of need; not mine, but other persons, as if they could conjure up this impulse of mine. I began to experience this expansion of body and mind more and more intensely. One night I did not sleep, but found myself floating quietly, like a small boat in a swiftly flowing river of thoughts. I floated and the thoughts sifted and eddied around my consciousness. I did not seem to mind the loss of sleep but felt myself cradled, embraced, resting in gentle awareness. It was a time when movement and stillness were at one a deep silence, more profound than any I had ever known. Gradually I perceived with some kind of hearing, inward not outward, much in the way I would hear the sound of the mantra in meditation, a sound so distant, so delicate and quiet that I could scarcely admit it was there. A tone, and then, a tone of voice. The tone and not the voice. There were words, but no sound. The silence had become words, perhaps in the way that ice melts or water turns to steam. The same fact with a different structure. Very gradually I came to distinguish a meaning, the noiseless syllables forming and reforming like crystals. The focus of my mind slowly gathered these, and there was a moment when I was aware of the sequence. Some part of me was astounded, some part familiar, as with one's own body. The impulse faded and focused, and became steady. Familiar, sweet words.

"Jo, Jo, I am here. We are all here, together. We are one, thou and I. Here is the core. Have no fear. I *am* always here, and always will be. This is your mind, this is my body. Your body and mind are also mine. This is love. I love you, embrace and enfold you. Tom, Tom".

"Yes, that is my name, the name that *you* know. Others I have that no man knows. Sleep now. I will come again".

So I slept then, and waking, remembered, knowing this voiceless sound, hearing an echo.

"Have no fear".

But I *was* afraid. Something in me had spoken, there would be surrender: everything. I was unable. I began to struggle, like a plant growing – I wasn't ripe, not quite. I felt pulled this way and that. I desperately longed for release, and once more the image of rescue came to my mind. I felt, in panic, that I was back in the same dream as before. I knew I would have to endure once more the pains of growth.

I thought to myself, and then said to the boys, "I will be able to manage this time. I'll not say or do anything that will send me into a hospital. I'll experience, but I will also sustain".

I'd been meditating every day and performing simple asanas. I was sure that whatever the processes of my mind in the coming sequence, that I would be strong enough to carry the stresses and eventually that they would dissolve and disperse of themselves.

Over a period of several weeks I found myself in a turmoil of desire; the physical aspect of this was consuming and powerful. I sought for reality and found fantasy. I resurrected Tom in my imagination, again and again. One day I was so convinced that he would come that when the front door opened and a man entered the room I screamed aloud, in an ecstasy of greeting and fear. It was one of my sons, and he was astounded and anxious at my reaction. At this time also I began to feel a great confusion in my will. I would begin an action and not be able to finish it, go across the room to fetch something and not remember what it was. Sit down again, only to get up at once and retrace my steps.

I wandered around the house not really remembering my errand … and then began to be drowsy, very heavy and sleepy at times in the day, but wakeful in the night so that often I didn't want to go to bed at all. I felt that the rescuer, the 'bridegroom' would come when I least expected him, and that I must be ready with my lamp alight.

I found I could not drive to my job without almost falling asleep at the wheel. When I got there, I begun to feel sleepy, a curiously heavy, drugged feeling. In the classroom I had to fight to stay awake. I went to the doctor and told him about this and my previous difficulties. He instructed me to stay at home and rest and advised a visit to the outpatient psychiatric clinic. I'd only been back at school one week. While I was there I'd noticed a hill opposite the school. It was obviously an ancient place; one could see a structure of terraces curving along the coarse hillside grass. I walked up there during the dinner hour and felt drawn there by its atmosphere. At the top I found a grove of enormous trees; scraggy, windswept ancient trees, very tall and gnarled, the only branches very close to the top, as if the wind had pruned away all surplus growth. One was larger than the others, a crucifix shape, the others a little smaller, and a crop of saplings.

I explored the area and found a rough circle and something resembling an arena. There were tree bodies lying, huge reclining figures, and the broad stumps from which they had been sawn. At intervals there were ancient stumps covered with grass. I looked and prodded the ground, pushing with my fingers into the rough mounds of grass which showed on the level areas, and found woody fibres underneath.

The trees had stood, it seemed, for many generations. A tree-henge. They were sweet chestnuts. These were introduced into this island by the Romans. I guessed that the hill itself and its earth-works were a much earlier fort. I looked around at the circle of hills, sea, and sky. Five counties, and a microcosm of life, man, and nature. Mountains of Monmouthshire to the north, to the south the Severn Sea: beyond the water, Devon and the Mendip Hills.

The village nudged the hillside a mile away, but a motorway swung around its base, a sweeping mile of elegant modern carriageway. Two schools with their brilliant green playing fields. The cooling towers of a power station

I looked across the Severn and saw in my mind's eye, Glastonbury. If you stood so that the three largest trees were in a straight line, your eye was directed there across the water.

My mind began to wander again. The warm September sun seduced me, and I lay down in a dip in the tussocky fragrant grass ...

> Thomas, the twin. A story unravelling in fragments. Jesus, a twin, an identical brother. That's how the plan was completed. The story about their meeting in the upper room was a double bluff, to make sure that they were both included in the record of events after the cross. Thomas had to undergo the wounds

as well, there had to be a completely authentic and convincing physical likeness. Hands, feet, and sides. No half measures. The wounds would be made in time to heal sufficiently for him to walk easily. Thomas had not only learned his role from his brother; he was the Christ also, a hidden incognito helper. He willingly resigned all his authority to his brother until this painful denouement. It was decided between them which would go to the cross and which would undergo the wounds at the hands of friends. A compulsive determination to make a happening which would arrest the imagination of generations to come and draw their attention to the teaching. With people who were used to violence and pain, the idea of bringing a man back to life after a death by torture would be, to use a modern term, a fantastic publicity (fantastic in the non-slang sense too).

There was a real possibility that the human mind could be jerked into a new evolutionary path, unstoppable, a qualitative change in the whole process of life. The impact on the imagination of this act of love would affect the germination of a dormant cell in the nature of man. The fact that some imaginations had already conceived of such a thing made it more likely to happen. The spontaneous growth process was already on the point of splitting apart to make a birth channel for just such an event. The unique individuals who found themselves impelled into action on this level could not help themselves once the sequence was begun. They were caught in a 'this thing is bigger than both of us' syndrome. In any case, they had surrendered the will to this spontaneous impetus and did not resist what appeared to them as a natural inevitable flow. They were the flow. (Not thy will, but thy will be done.)

Jesus/Thomas knew himself as the flow, and the source of that flow. His awareness perceived the connection, the synchronicity between apparently unconnected factors – the relationship between things and people. Nature itself supported the way his mind imagined the course of events. He found what he proposed to do he could in fact do, precisely and with exact timing. Judas. Yes, Judas had the hardest task of all (0 felix culpa). Without him, nothing. The best beloved friend would accept the fate of a traitor. He would know what would be said about him, and have to hold his tongue. When it came to the point he could only kiss his friend and reach for oblivion as quickly as possible. Thus, Thomas – in the garden, so early in the morning (Jesus still lying in his tomb – but that's another story). And Thomas in the inner room; Thomas on the lakeside. It made no difference which one it was. Certainly there was something, a physical difference; and another thing too. Thomas was experiencing on an empathetic level, a transcendent connection with his brother; his mind, diving within, had met with the spirit of his twin and was re-united with him. Already his other half in physical terms he now became him on an altogether deeper level. (Tom, oh, Tom, I love you!) Or was it Thomas on the cross and Jesus in the garden? (Jesus, o Jesus, I love you!)

Thomas and Joseph left the quiet village of Arimathea and made their way to the coast. It had become urgently necessary to depart from Palestine. A man with scars on his hands and feet was a marked man (just that) in a county governed by Roman military rule. They were joined by Joseph's wife, Ann, and his daughter Joanna. They embarked on a coastal trader for the long sea journey to Malta. From there they joined another ship for the hazardous northward sailing for the misty, and to them, highly mysterious island of Britain.

They arrived after many weeks and saw the soft outlines of the unknown shore, the south coast, and the Roman town of Dorchester. The ship came into a

Fugue

small quiet harbour, a little further west. The travellers went on alone and looked around them, aware of the freshness of the air, the scent of sea grasses. Saw the gulls swooping low on the water, and the green rolling downs ahead.

It was July, a warm day. Joseph had been here before. He knew the way, how to follow the old straight tracks from hill to hill, standing stones marking the narrow well-trodden path. They would go north. Losing no time they began walking. Passing a village not far from the shore they bartered for some clothing – rough, homespun tunics and cloaks so that they would be indistinguishable from other folks in this quiet land.

Glastonbury. The ancient hill rose in the distance. Joseph pointed it out. Thomas had found the long walk painful, as his feet, though healed, tired easily. Now would come a peaceful time, a country life. He would settle down with Joanna making a livelihood as a carpenter, ploughs and yolks, tables and benches, carve a little, and a harp for the winter evenings. And he would walk in the hills, meditate and teach the country people what he knew of the love of God and show them how to unfold that love from within themselves.

A few years of peace. Children, sturdy and strong, twin boys and a little girl, a new way of life, natural and free. The people in the little farms and cottages would gather at their hearth and a warmth came to them there. Once, when they were talking of the great powers that love could work in a man, a wind blew upon them, and each one saw what looked like a flame, a brightness above the heads of the others.

Then the Romans came. They marched up to Thomas's door, and he came out to them. They searched the house and the small holding from end to end. They looked at his scars, and then took him away. They took him to Caerleon, a camp north of the great river, and

Time Out of Mind

there he stayed, chained to others like him, felons and rebels and other outcasts.

One day in March they took him with a dozen others, marched them along the road east, beside the Severn sea, crossing the River Usk, reaching the hill of execution.

The sun rose high. The trees large, tall and bare in the cold wind, the channel waters silver grey, flecked with brief patches of sun as the western wind blew the clouds aside. South, the hills and Glastonbury (a weeping wife and children).

So the nails pierced the hands and feet for the second time, and the trees stood in the wind. Just another day's work, not even worth recording. The bodies were taken down after three days and burned on the spot. Rough graves a few feet down the hill on a level space … it was Wotan Day.

I lay with the sun drenching my eyelids. The flow of words and images in my head stopped and I was back again, here on this hillside, two thousand years away. Why did I have such thoughts; I didn't ask to think them, they just came into my head. Why these?

I returned to this hill several times. One morning I woke before sunrise and seemed to hear Tom calling me. It was late September and cool. I went out to the car and drove the twelve miles to that place. I took off my shoes and started to walk up the rough track in my bare feet. I expected to see him in the dim light. The grasses rustled in the dawn breeze. I went to the top and stared up at the gaunt branches of the chestnut trees.

Just a slight movement there. A deep silence. I sat with my back to the biggest tree and looked out over the Severn River.

I must surrender, give in, let go. Tom was not a body, a physical body, a man; he would not walk over the grass now and take my hand. He was here nevertheless, within and without, an environment in which I existed, which extended and shaped me. I could not avoid him or deny him in any way (behold the handmaid). I went to the edge of the hill, looked down at the quiet road and the village beyond. The sun was coming up. On the way down, about half way, I kicked something lying on the ground. I found a tennis ball at my feet. It was split open, like a peapod, and I held it in my hand. Like that deflated bladder. A bit of rubbish, a leftover. A dead body. Nothing to it. I did let go, just then. I gave in – or out. The space in that old ball and the whole space outside, to the boundaries of the galaxy – all one; I didn't need to go seeking for Tom or expect him to come searching for me. Our identities had fused. What was there was also here.

>Foxes have holes and birds have nests
>Returning now I take my rest
>Hearts ease to ride thus, two abreast,
>Birds gliding and skimming the wind
>Born on the slip-stream of spirit
>Never looking behind
>Not fearless or frozen, but feeling
>Extending, expanding
>Breasting the barriers boundless
>Breaking bursting the ancient thongs
>Bonding the broken, the vessel
>Most excellent, fragile pulsating
>0 thou, thou heart-plucker
>String-puller, bow-bender;
>Send, sound, sunder me
>Good-ridden, God-riven, for-given,
>Found

Back home I was plunged into domestic activity – still off sick. I got busy in the house and garden; the pears were ripening on the tree, apples too, and the tall sunflowers were fructifying to deep brown centres. Everything, every fruit, flower, plant; every object and person became for me a symbol, with its own mystic reality. Every word almost; numbers, shapes, colours. I seemed then like an animal listening for a movement on the wind.

Language especially became lively for me. Layer upon layer of connection and meaning. It was as if it had a molecular structure like the rest of nature. Just as one could not *see* the atoms and their patterns in space, making up the solidities and spaces in one's environment; and of necessity living and moving at the level of perception, at eye level, so also one lived at 'ear' level when it came to words. It gradually had become apparent to me that my ear/mind took in language on more than one level, and though each level was connected, the deeper levels were, as it were, analogous; a mythical version of what the surface was doing. (I find this happens as I write things down; the sequence breaks up into these levels and swings between them; sometimes the boundaries are clear, sometimes they just blend together. Whether the reader can sustain concentration in and out of these fluctuations I don't know!)

I went to the psychiatric clinic in the hospital and talked to the doctor, a learned professor. He listened attentively and offered to read my poetry, which I left with him. But he offered me no advice.

My thoughts had now reached a pitch of intensity about one particular thing. It was on a practical level of experience, and I couldn't avoid the implications these impressions had for me. I had, on that first 'trip' four years earlier, come to the conclusion that there were no coincidences but that *all* happenings were in some way connected. I had noticed, then as now, that my thoughts and actions were related to spontaneous events outside my voluntary control. I responded quite naturally to the primitive impulse to relate the unrelated; I made causal connections, I experienced synchronicity. If I had an experience like making a negative value judgement about someone in the room with me, I found myself hurting myself. I'd knock my elbow, burn my finger, break a glass. Whatever I did that was destructive had a destructive effect on me, either thought-wise or by actions. And likewise, I observed that when I hit on a growing, liberating sequence of thoughts and activities, these produced a spontaneous response in the environment. Quite literally, a bell would ring – I tried to explain this to one or two friends and was plainly not understood, and thought to be freaking again. I wasn't sure if I understood it either, but I recognised the actual experience. I could describe it to myself another way. If my thoughts were very strong and demanding at a given moment, my coordination would lose its stability – for a second I was not paying attention, and then I would hurt myself. Thus, a man who tripped up in a wood and 'by accident' broke his leg when he fell over a root *could* be aware of the sequence of thoughts which had caused his downfall. If they were pulling his attention away from his present activity, it would be well for him to know what kind of thoughts they were and pay some attention to them. I found that such events drew attention, myself to my *self*, to some things in my mind I did well to notice for my future well-being.

The most difficult, disastrous bit was now budding up to the surface. I'd been half awake to it before. Now it was in full focus, and I felt trapped. All I had thought, felt, and been added up to one thing, and I just didn't want to know.

I was more afraid of this than of anything ever before. *It was a taboo of terrifying dimensions.* In some quite definite, absolute way, on one of the levels of the mind I was experiencing, I felt myself, me, my identity to be one and the same as God. I felt this as a spontaneous necessity. I didn't want to be God. I couldn't see how I could be just that, it was altogether too difficult. There was no way of stopping the thought. It was there. I tried to forget it and push it aside. I couldn't get rid of it. It was there, and there it stayed. I could only say to myself again and again, "Why pick on me?" I didn't want this, I didn't – if you'd asked me, I'd have *said no, I can't, I can't. No.* And then, desperately seeking an alternative, I said, *I resign. God can't resign! I want to die, I want to sleep; oblivion.* God can't die or be in oblivion. I had some pills from the doctor. I'd only taken four, and then put them aside – they made me feel blanketed, foggy. I got out the bottle and thought about it. If I was dead then perhaps that would be like Tom's death, produce a new, growing development in my environment. I could abdicate, and something good would happen.

I was alone in the house. The need to make a decision was more and more urgent. To me at every point of perception it was true. I, myself, this fragile, nervous creature, female, widowed, middle-aged, mad, was also inescapably *God*. Everything that had happened before was child's play. This evidently was grown-up stuff. I didn't take the pills. I went to bed.

The next day I wanted to hide, but I had to get on with it. The feeling uppermost was isolation. I felt, talking to family, friends, that I had a mask on and that everything I was saying was lies, a cover-up, a pretence which someone, sooner or later would see through. I decided that evening I couldn't keep it up. I must tell someone. But that could be a disaster, I'd be locked up again. It was an impossible hubris.

Fred, my poet friend, was staying with me. I tried to put it into words, and it was coming out all wrong – *this is my mind which is given for you* – I was mad, but I knew I was, and I had to be willing to be, and be split and torn (Oh, God, all I want is to be a woman, have a man to love and to love me, to have more kids and live, work, make love. Oh, God, such simple, sweet things – I'm not a masochist, I don't want all this pain – please, *please!*).

We were in the kitchen, and it was close and stuffy. I had just come to the point of actually telling him in so many words, when my voice was overwhelmed by a shattering crash of thunder. It seemed to be right overhead. I tried to go on, but the noise was deafening, and there seemed no point in trying to compete. I made mugs of coffee and decided to shut up. I would have to go on as I could and leave the rest to nature. I felt sure of one thing. Whatever was happening, *I would eventually understand it.* The knowledge would grow naturally and I would not always be afraid and hurt. It had to work out, I would somehow turn this terrifying impulse of my mind into something equable, normal, balanced, creative.

> I have been sleeping, like a princess
> How many years I cannot tell
> This soul I have lies like a frozen seed
> For centuries entombed, like dust
> Then comes to life, like light
> A fingers touch, then slowly, surely
> Silently it comes, the flower, the fire
> Enflaming all, warming all worlds
> Balm for my wounds, and beacon
> For my mind …

The sense of exposure continued, remorselessly. I felt, when I went out, that everyone knew, not intellectually but deeper down. It seemed people stared at me. But equally, and often, people made it easy for me; traffic lights changed to green – I seemed to be surrounded by a very

Fugue

special kindness from people I'd never seen before. I began to say, in my head, Tom, Tom, I can't do this, any of it. You must do it with me, for me. I resign, surrender, give over, everything, the whole bloody works! And it worked. It began to be easier.

> I want to talk to you, Tom,
> Mr Eliot, sir, where are you walking
> I have been stirring the morning air
> With my friend, Mr Thomas, Tom,
> We were talking, strolling along
> The tow path by the Thames
> Thomas I said, shall we begin In the beginning.
> You said, there is yet more reality,
> Truth beyond truth
> We pass
> Understanding, it remains
> Earthbound like Prometheus.
> I left it one November day
> (I remember it was like the spring, green,
> The sun and the roses flowering)
> In-words and out-words, don't tell me,
> I don't know, the flight was
> Fugitive at first, last gasping
> Sob-streaked, supersonic,
> Then, star-leaping came the
> Projectile of the self in vaulting
> Parabolic curve, the boomerang
> Returns to the hand of the aboriginal
> Man-woman, who made it,
> Threw it, and slew with it the bird
> Of paradise …
> Only stunned it seems. The head
> Lifts slowly, and the jewelled eyes
> Open. Wings widen, showing colours
> Rainbowed like a torrent in the sun
> We will take this home to the children,

We said, it was a phoenix
Anyway, and could not have died.
Tom, you must not let me wander off
Like that, I was trying to say
In the same tone of voice you had
("*The common one, without vulgarity*")
I wanted to say it so often before –
I tried once, too soon, and a crash
Of thunder almost crowned me
Scared me out of my mind
(And not for the first time – I'm frightened
Of cows as well)
When I woke up that new time
I knew, I could not un-know
That further thing that none of you
Would ever actually say.
So I said it. And became.
I said it, it was so, and would
Have been so if you had said it
Only you didn't – not quite
I said: I am
I am that is, he, she, and we,
Tom, I am Thou, and thou
(How did you manage to hide it, and why)
Art the one (I will whisper your every day
Name, silently in case someone is peeping
(God) l think that plenty of other folk
Are perfectly well aware of the fact
But it's too remarkably embarrassing
To admit it – in so many words.
So the men look like it, with beards,
Long hair, or sandals, the girls
Lengthen their skirts and their hair
Too.
But we're all of us Jesus, one way
Or the other (or will be)

Fugue

> That very identity split a billion
> Milky ways and more, the arms of the
> Galaxy swing out immensely from
> The centre, where am I, Oh
> Where am I, spinning and
> Yet still. How strange a truth
> To tell, that this man
> Tom, who loved this woman, Jo,
> Becomes this centre because of this
> Love, this ordinary domestic
> Love, this human thing, this
> Life is, the world to come
> Become.

One Sunday in October, I took Esther across the town to an outlying suburb. A christening, followed by a party. I was God-mother. Well, that seemed good to be, in this new role. It was a great party and a happy gathering of Tom's kinsfolk. When it was over I got the kids and we climbed in the VW bus. It wouldn't start. I'd got used to that lately. I got out again and used an old trick to get the starter working, I got hold of the fly-belt and gave it a turn by hand. I signalled to my friend, one of the Mums, to try the engine. No go. I tried twice more. The fourth time the engine started; while I still had my hands on the fan belt. There was a sharp stabbing pain. I looked at my hands. My little finger was missing (no remission of sins without shedding of blood …). Frodo of the Nine Fingers. I wanted it back, my finger. I looked for it in the dark, underneath the engine. I couldn't find it.

I went back to the house and called out, "I've lost my finger – can you come and help find it?"

I ended up in casualty having it stitched. No finger turned up. I went home with a big bandage and a couple of painkillers. It really didn't hurt as much as I expected. I slept OK.

> Posted missing, believed dead?
> Lying somewhere
> In a gutter, or a garter,

Time Out of Mind

Perhaps even in a gaiter
(My spare tyre of course)
Though VW vans keep spares under the front seat.
Spare fingers and nails? Very handy, handy Andy.
Come and find it for me then, and
We'll put it to good use, no doubt.
Preserve it in aspic, or a glass case.
Make mince pies for Xmas, or just see
How long it lasts without benefit
Of a deep freezer.
I wonder how much workman's compensation
A fairy godmother gets for losing half a finger
While on active service?
After all, I had intended to learn
To play the harp, the sackbut and the crumhorn,
Let alone the recorder
Supposing I, a widow, had used
That favourite finger for masturbation and other
Innocent pleasures.
No, let us be frank
Its sweetest charm was: to stroke the innocent cheek,
The babies' brows, noses, lips – to dip
In stews and soufflés, cheesecakes and such,
To taste and see the flow and flavour
For my guests.
And the last upward stretch of the leaping scale,
The arpeggios I have yet to learn on my Welsh harp
Which I will fetch *today*

(A harpist does not use the little finger ...) I woke up early with a plan in my head. I would go to the harp-maker and buy me a harp. My attention was on my hands; so that was what I needed to do. Use them. I was offered a lift to drive up into the valley, to the little village under the Garth Mountain, There was a quiet atmosphere that day, and I set out feeling a little excited, rather like a child going to the sea-side. Going north, the road passes the big mental hospital and then out on to a dual-carriageway, the hills of Glamorganshire spread out, and straight ahead the wooded slope above the village of Pentyrch and on it the fairytale shape of Castle Coch. This day there were vast clouds, great entities of vapour streaming out from horizon to horizon, the arc of the sky filled with power and with light.

A hail storm hit the road, blinding the windscreen for a moment, rattling on the roof of the car; giant flakes spiralling over our heads. We didn't speak – we were caught in this apex of cloud, sky, mountain. Without warning I was projected out of my own familiar space.

I was beside myself. An expansion of the mind; the skull felt as if it had opened somehow, and all the contents were streaming out into this splendour of light. I felt a physical bliss, piercing, pulsating, a rising crescendo of sensation, not erotic, but somehow like that. If it was like anything it was like a climax of physical love, a magnificent orgasm. But it wasn't that. The feeling of body and mind soared, then a vibration of sound somewhere, a high bell-like infinite sound, very fine and very clear, attenuated. It was as if I was a telescope, body and mind, and that I was being focused, turned towards a brilliant light which burst upon me in full flood for a moment. Some white seabirds swung across the road, bright against the clouds, and soared high. I felt like them, with them. Light, airborne, higher soaring, and higher. My mind burst like an exploding shell in a spasm of radiance, whiter than dove's wings; a sound in my head, a note higher and sweeter and more distant than the pitch of words to tell, hovering, wind-like, a kite-bird. Bliss, blossoming in showers of white and gold. (Hosanna to the son of David, David, David.) Then we came to the turning, and I was returned.

The road went through woods, winding the hillside. The harp-maker's cottage, stone-built into the mountain. He came to greet us, a gnarled tree-trunk of a man, broad and bearded. Wisdom and skill his milieu, coming from him like woodland breezes. He didn't have a harp in the workshop, but his son had one, a small Welsh Celtic harp. He never played it now; perhaps he would be willing to sell it; he preferred football. It was fetched down from the house, and my heart beat faster. It was small, few strings on it, black with a natural wood sounding board. Beautiful. We agreed on a price and within two days I was the possessor of a fully strung harp. It had the sound of a bell, like the ones

I heard ringing in my head. I had to tune it myself. Its creator confessed he could not tune a harp, having no ear for pitch.

I put the harp, the harp of David, on the bookshelf. Once again the house was empty. I lay down and for a long time floated on the thought of that place in the sky where I'd been for a moment. I began to cry. Tears welled up and fell down into my ears. I began to feel an anguish as deep and full as the crown of the hill is high, my head felt like a crown of thorns. I couldn't stop – the tears were like vomit, like spit, pouring out. There was no escaping. I didn't understand. I couldn't believe in myself crying like that. It didn't seem to be about anything. I wasn't crying because 'I' was dead, it felt more as if 'I' *was* sadness, tears, all the tears in the world. No comfort, no consolation, I felt I would have to lie there and weep forever, to never stop. What was happening to me? *Oh, God, why pick on me? Why does it have to be me?* Dusk came, then darkness. The whole of my mind and body used up – I was used, abused. I recognised one thing very sharply; that myself was a vessel, a channel. A point of exit, or a vent-hole. Pressure was pouring out through me; I simply had to experience. But like a glass jar, full of corrosive acid, that pouring could not destroy me and it would be refilled eventually with wine and with flowers. I got up in the dark and went out into the garden. I collected four wine bottles on the way and some milk bottles as well. It was a mild night, a little windy. I threw the bottles at the dry stone wall behind the house, with all my strength. As each one shattered and the sound scattered and echoed into the quietness I felt relief, and again, again, and I felt release.

> I know a pain when I see one
> I have had so many of my own
> This pain is as old as the rivers and fountains
> I also have been there alone
> You feel the wounds of the world
> Your voice speaks never a word
> This sorrow enfolds the stars and the mountains
> You also reap your reward
> Thou surrendering life for a friend,
> Embracing the world without end,

> Thou that vessel and thou the flower it contains
> Thou breaking and making a mend
> Sower and reaper to blend.

Next day the house was suddenly full of folk. The boys returned from their long ride to Spain and back. (The first time I had been without them.) They brought welcome and booze and were as brown as berries. Talked for hours in the kitchen, glasses full and flowing. I drank not too much but rather too mixed and went glowing to bed. I woke with a terrible headache. A blinder. And it was my day to go to the clinic. I was sick.

By eleven my appointment was due and I felt weak and shaky. I pulled myself into my clothes and out of the house and in to the outpatient waiting hall. I took my harp so I'd have something to do and take my mind off my stomach. I felt like showing it to people, to my doctor. I was sitting with other patients in the same category: mental. And I began to play Welsh folk tunes. The result was intense delight, almost a party. Everyone around relaxed and started talking to each other. Waiting was no problem.

My turn to go in and be seen. I had something important to tell him. About my finger, and the harp, and my trip, high and low these last few days. Above all I wanted to tell him about my finger; it was growing again. I was absolutely certain – I'd seen for myself. It would grow and replace itself because I wanted it to. It would be a growth like cancer is, but it would be creative, not destructive. The cells would form and reconstruct my missing bit. It was several centimetres larger already, after five days. Crabs could do this so why shouldn't human beings? I felt excited, like a child again, with something great to look forward to. My enthusiasm was real, overflowing. I warmed to the idea and expressed it forcefully, as I would any piece of good news. It was true.

The doctor looked at me thoughtfully and said, "I see".

I talked some more.

He said, "I know".

Finally he said, "I want you to come in to hospital for a short stay, for observation mainly. It's a small ward, part of our teaching unit. Would you be willing to do that?"

I agreed instantly. I had no fear this time. This man gave me confidence, not directly, but I felt I would not be imposed upon, and I was assured that the door would be open. Next day I got a letter asking me, inviting me, very courteously, to present myself for admission the following week.

I felt very relaxed, happy. The weather for October was spring-like and mellow. I sat in the sun, cooked tasty meals, and even looked forward to the hospital as a valid new experience. For a few days all sorrows were forgotten. Back of my mind the wind hovered. God hovered. I fell in love again (was I ever out of it – it was a state of mind) which meant that this ever-present Tom-ness got focused on to a here and now person. I wrote a tragi-comic love letter to my friend and asked him to sleep with me. I wanted to be with a man. I really did. It had been so long. A reply came quite promptly, declining the offer. I felt restless, I wanted some lively action. Something to do, somewhere to go. (I'd be in hospital soon.)

> "To a Missing Limb"
> A small, innocent portion
> Parted with for a time.
> A small loss, so small
> That the heart aches
> Throbs, tears fall for
> Limbs flung wide
> In Ireland
> And all other
> Startling forms of
> Folly
> "A fool who persists in
> His folly will become wise".
> Blake begs us to be
> "'Ware, win wisdom now,
> And not another day"
> Come now, my friends,
> Be not 'reived by this
> Chance, but let's go

Fugue

Softly, meditatively together,
Bring in the quiet revolution
The grandeur, gargantuan
Splendour of life.
Split sorrow
Split sides
Splice splintered bones
And join me,
Jo
Why don't we just grow new ones?

My finger hurt – that's because it was growing. Growing pains. I decided to hitchhike to a doctor I knew of in Somerset. He lived near Glastonbury. I put Rueben's fireman's jacket on, complete with brass-buttons, a long brown-haired wig over my short crop, and bright scarlet knee-length breeches over heavy white tights. I was in disguise; a pilgrim. I got a lift almost at once all the way. My chauffeur was an Irish labourer. Before I got out I threw my arms around his neck and kissed him because he was a man.

I was nearly there – Glastonbury. I got another lift, and soon saw the stump, the ancient mound. My finger began to throb painfully. It seemed to be swelling, bursting, as if to greet that twin shape on the hill. It responded independently, like an erection. All the time I was within sight of that Glastonbury Tor my finger stump burned with energy.

I told the doctor about it growing. He showed no surprise, examined it, dressed it, and told me to go in peace. I felt consoled and validated. At least someone took me seriously ... my finger, yes, it was my finger. That part of me which had died was as much as the whole – the part was the whole. Now I was in two places at once. Was that the meaning of my going up and going down?

My soul had gone to heaven and then to hell, and was it now resurrected?

Tom's death had the same effect. When he had gone I had followed him in my mind and would not let go, until I rejoined him.

How would my finger grow? It could have a different form now.

Tom Thumb. Another self would manifest there. At first a shape, vaguely head-shaped, and then a miniscule brow, a cranium, delicately crowned with fine downy hair, small buds on the surface breaking through, orifices, eyes; but only vestigial forms where nose and mouth would have been; a long period with lids closed, as infinitely complex a computer is built, with its microscopic details. Several months, and then, one morning I wake, and the eyes open, bright as birds, and as tiny. Vivid and sparkling with laughter. And from that other Self flows such a magic of sweet conversation that the heart dances. No words of sound, but the inner mind speaks; two minds with but a single thought, or not quite, because there is a dialectic, it is a non-dual wholeness of intention. It is myself and yet it is not myself. It is the Other. My brother/sister, man (Br = Brahman).

I was reading in bed. A blue-bottle fly, a vivid metallic greenish black, with five legs and feelers, marvellously developed eyes like tiny black peppercorns, settled on my book. It moved with authority across the page and settled on a word: manifest. Well, little fly, you must be a relative of mine, I said. Absolute and relative. My finger is absolute. The missing bit. The lost remnant, dropped in a gutter, mated with a fly. The maggots breeding from that morsel of decay now spawning a family of thoroughbred flies. Queen of the Flies.

"Oh, fly, I greet you. Now I know who you are I will treat you with greater respect. And if I am driven to despatch you I shall send you, with affection, to a higher sphere of life – a bird or a bee, maybe. Yes, and when my finger wakes I will have eyes in the back of my head like you. I've only to put my hand there and I will see you with my own eyes, or into my pocket or my bag like a little torch to search for a lost article. An antenna".

Already it seemed to me that the other self was permeating my consciousness. The ghost part of myself an inescapable, permanent influence. Perhaps a part of my body, flesh, blood, and bone had to die, to bridge the gap. The awareness of mind could connect with that further stage, but only the state of one's body could complete it. I could not go beyond this life of mine without being physically dead. A contradiction in terms. The loss of my finger-self was a tiny, factual link. (I have noticed that other people I know who have lost parts of their body become qualitatively different from other people – some are greatly distressed by this and feel disorientated, isolated.)

Fugue

A long time ago, very long, another sequence, a time of darker than dark. The convex image, the underside. Figures moving and talking together; one talking the others listening. A man with long hair, wrapped in a woollen cloak. His conversation is a criminal offence, punishable by death. He speaks of love, freely felt and acted out, in a land where such a state of mind is regarded as a weakness. (My strength is made perfect in weakness.) A meal is eaten in haste, a loving farewell before the disaster. The man, Mereu, is arrested, bullied, beaten. When his clothes are torn from his back, his tormentors are amazed to find that this is a woman. She is also pregnant, close to time, so she is whipped with rods and raped as well. Then nailed to a post like an inverted T, both hands above the head, the legs parted wide and nailed to the crossbar. Thus she gives birth to twins, a boy and a girl, while the executioners roll on the grass, laughing uncontrollably. The new born infants are thrust into a bag and taken to a baby kennel, a sort of stable where captive women have to suckle the young. They are chained to the walls, fed like animals, their punishment for showing a weakness for love.

Some of them have been suckling babies here for twelve years and more. The babies crawl on the deep litter. At nine months old they will be taken to a training litter where they will be made to walk. The woman is taken down from the crossbar and walked into a stone cavern. She is provided with a loaf and a bottle of wine and is told that the cave will be opened in one month, at the full moon, and that if she is alive she will be free.

Her impulse to survive and recover her babies is painful. She gives herself minute amounts of the bread and wine, and collects, eats, and drinks all her excrement. When this has gone she begins to eat herself, gnawing her fingers, sucking her own blood ...

I've always bitten my nails and chewed my fingers when under any kind of pressure. The day came when I was to go into hospital. It seemed quite an ordinary event. I felt calm, even happy. It would be good to have a rest, away from all the bustle and responsibility. There would be a comfortable bed; perhaps a kind of convalescence. And I would be able to talk about some of these strange and difficult things. They would take me seriously, listen.

I found the ward bright and comfortable and the door was open. I felt quite at ease and talked to other patients and to the nurses. I offered to wash up and make tea, and was encouraged to do so. All was well. I meditated as usual. I did this every day, morning and evening. I was aware that this kept a thread of connection, however tenuous, through all the swings my mind was capable of taking – twixt and 'tween the layers of its nature. It was like Ariadne's thread enabling me to ravel the twisting tunnels to the den of the minotaur and return in safety to the outside world. And I'd found that the minotaur was myself, only with a mask on. What a joke – JO-OK?

The first shock came in the evening. I was reading quietly in bed, about nine forty-five; if sleep didn't come I would be still, and allow my mind to follow any pattern of thought that came.

A nurse came with pills. "Here are your sleepers".

"I don't take sleeping pills".

She looked at me sharply, as if I'd said something offensive. "Well, you'll have to take them here. We can't have you tramping around at night disturbing the patients. The staff have to walk through this room on their rounds at night, you'll need them so that you don't wake".

It all seemed quite illogical. "I'll just keep them beside me then, so I can take one if I need it".

"Oh no, I must see you swallow them – you might be tempted to save them all up".

I could see I wasn't getting anywhere, and I didn't feel like making a scene, so I swallowed them. I felt a small anger rising but put it aside. I went on reading, using the small light over the bed. "Well", I thought, "they won't work for twenty minutes or so, I'll have time to read a bit further".

Two sentences later came a sharp interruption. "Light out now, Mrs Thomas".

It was ten o'clock. I protested gently, pointing out that my pattern of sleep was totally different, midnight to seven a.m., or at any rate about six or seven hours, difficult to alter in one night. The rejoinder was that the sleeping pills solved that problem for everyone.

My valuables, clothes, and personal items had been taken earlier, listed and locked away. Deprived of that semblance of domesticity I suddenly felt alienated and physically restless for the first time since entering the hospital. I turned out the light and silently wept in the darkness. Was I to be punished like a naughty child, or was I here to resolve the problems of identity, to learn how to live with myself in a better way? My confidence was badly damaged (I knew temporarily, but that didn't make it less painful).

Next morning I woke early feeling drugged and heavy. Breakfast was friendly and good and I felt human again. After breakfast came the inevitable line-up for pills. I felt a mild panic rising but got control over the past and enquired quite serenely what kind I was being given. Largactil.

"I had some rather disastrous after-effects from taking those last time – is there any alternative?"

A quick check was made, the doctor consulted. Yes, I could have something else. So I swallowed my pills and went down to the occupational therapy department.

A young man in a white coat, tall, with long dangling arms, appeared to be in charge. He showed me where to find some materials, paper, paints, brushes. I joined six imperial sheets together, pushed two tables likewise, and started. Later a young woman in a white coat came and talked about what I was doing. I began to realise that I couldn't distinguish which were patients and which were hospital staff. The young man proved to be a fellow patient. Neil. He had four fingers missing from one hand. I worked several days, and more and more noticed that everyone I talked to resembled someone I knew. I had a déjà vu experience with people. It was not so much on the level of imagination or feeling. I found it to be observably so.

I thought, "If I live long enough I shall recognise my kinship with the whole human family as a reality, and feel like behaving in a way which truthfully reflects that relationship".

A distinguished older man sat beside me while we had elevenses. I felt respect, as from a daughter to father. I was attracted too, in much the same vein. I wondered if he was an incognito psychotherapist, keeping contact with patients, listening to their problems, offering wisdom, insight and help. No, he turned out to be another patient.

It becomes clear that the patient-to-patient empathy, which grows up when the atmosphere is warm and friendly, where there is work to do and to share, was a vital part of mental growth and health; I began to talk more and more with other patients and to worry less about talking to doctors (which was a rare occasion anyway). But for the pills. I began to have double vision and with this, a feeling of great unease. I recognised that this depression, even anguish would pass, and that it was a reaction of my nervous system to a very powerful drug. I was having a bad trip. On the next days I fought against the unreality of this state of mind, but realised I could also learn something. The unreality, though drug induced, could also be a valid process if I could sustain the learning process. The double vision changed everyone's faces. I saw people with their noses twisted, parts of their features torn away, mutilated. Everyone's eyes appeared to be full of pain. Even my sons' and daughter's features were torn and disfigured. *I was in a hospital for people suffering from the effects of radiation. An atomic holocaust.*

Four or five days and I could bear it no longer. I was allowed home for a weekend. Somehow my pills were forgotten. I could have had a supply to take with me. The effects were still in my system, however. I had hoped for relief in my own home, but that was an illusion, as I could only react from within my own dilemma.

So when I found the home in domestic chaos, the kitchen littered with dirty crockery, the sink full, and stale food lying around, I let loose all the stress of the last days. All the anger and frustration leaped to the surface. I grabbed a poker and began to thrash the most solid thing I could see – the top of the Aga cooker. The sparks flew from the cast-steel plates and the kettle handle flew off! I was the poker, the hot-plate, the kettle. I flew off the handle, I sparked, I beat the hell out of it, like a blacksmith with an anvil. I was Thor (Thursday's child has far to go).

Later that day I made a burnt offering by way of reconciliation to my homestead god. I put my broken wedding ring, a silver cross, made by a Mexican monk, on which was engraved AMEN; the A had no crossbar. The A became an inverted U. ΛMEN. And the silver figure of crucified Christ from a crucifix, together with the crossbar. That left me with the post on the wooden base. These metals, silver and gold, I consigned to the melting influence of the furnace. I felt I'd done it before sometime (and I remembered the mission of Frodo, Gollum, and Sam, and how the Ring of Power melted away in the fires of the Crack of Doom). I looked in the ash pan for a metallic fragment but found no trace.

Back in the ward I was called to a case conference. A psychiatrist and many students were present. I was asked about my experience with the missing finger. I think I told them everything, or almost everything, but not about the God bit. That was too embarrassing. I was asked the date of my night of sorrows and it was pointed out with some stir of interest that that date had been a full moon. Wednesday, 20th October 1970. I was evidently a classic example of a lunatic. I asked them why it should be this way.

The answer came. "There is some disturbance in the brain chemistry". So I was tripping, not on drugs (although I tended to do so on hospital drugs) but on something to do with my own electromagnetic system, some secretion or metabolic function, self-engendered, involuntary. But still *me* doing it; as natural to me as my menstruation – another moon cycle.

I was allocated to a woman doctor to continue the conversation. At intervals I would talk with her for some time. *This was something quite different* – here was a person who not only listened but could also relate. Her own experience empathetic with mine. She was giving me her reality in response to mine. A new and joyful stimulus. I told her about Tom – she told me about her only child run over and killed on his fourth birthday. I invited her home at the weekend and she came. We had supper; she had committed herself to validate me, and she did just that. I believed in my own experience and for the first time felt quite sure that all that was happening would be fruitful for the future. This madness of mine would prove to have been a growing experience of learning and unfolding. A valid tool, useful equipment of understanding through which I would find better routes of communication through many levels of awareness. Once experienced, no area of the mind would be a danger, fearful, or mindless.

> In sharp barbs, spears, and spikes
> A bell rings shrilly and then
> A woman is at our door.
> Her hand is bleeding too
> Her broken pane, her broken
> Palm, home, husband
> Reflected in her shattered face,
> Transparent like the glass, but
> Look, the pane is gone,
> Our hands pass through
> Out into air and the warm
> Rain, the wind blowing
> From the dark Welsh mountains:
> It will soon be day

I had a few more days left as an inpatient. I wrote some poetry then and played my harp. The day came for me to visit the outpatients accident clinic for my little finger to be inspected. I was certain my stump had grown. While waiting I had a chance to look at the X-ray, I had a remarkable shock. The negative showed that only the top joint was missing. I had visualised my finger at the time of the accident as having two joints missing. My conviction of growth had been the result of a hallucination. I felt once again, deflated. *Very* flattened!

Back in the ward, that evening I settled in front of the TV to watch a special United Nations Day performance of the Ninth Symphony of Beethoven. Most of the patients were in bed early, or sitting talking. I listened, enthralled, and lost myself in the music. My eyes played tricks – beautiful auras appeared around the players, green, blue, purple. I was hearing the last few bars of the end of the Third Movement, blissfully wondering what colours would accompany the entry of the human voice into this music when a voice behind me said, "Come along now … ten o'clock, you know …"

A hand reached forward and turned off the TV. I never had time to think. I exploded like a bomb. "You can't *do that – it's an unspeakable insult.* How *dare you*!"

Just as I spoke these words with violent emotional emphasis, there was a loud report outside the window, a crashing sound. The nurse tried to explain about rules for lights out and I was preparing to argue with her when we were interrupted by the arrival of a wheelchair pushed by a young male nurse. In it was a pretty girl, a student nurse who I'd come to like a lot. Her name was Esther, same as my daughter. She was holding a wet cloth to her head; it was bloody and she was very pale.

"I was driving up just a minute ago", said the man. "The tyre burst and we ended up against a tree. She's hit her head quite badly – a bit concussed".

Beethoven was forgotten in the necessity of this new event. But I had an irresistibly strong feeling that my outburst of anger, my stress, had something to do with the bursting of that tyre, and I resolved to observe future phenomena of this kind, a curious transference of stress across invisible boundaries.

I discovered that the hospital had a woodwork shop. I got permission to use it, and brought a piece of wood in from the garden at home. A greengage tree had been cut down the year before. It had not fruited for thirteen years and was taking up space, so we chopped it down. I found a Y-forked section, with the bark intact.

Carving was a delight and I worked at it every day. I was transferred to the day-patients unit. Slept at home. I noticed something new. It puzzled me at first, and then I accepted it as one would a sneeze, a sigh, a desire to laugh or cry. It was this. The glow of warmth I earlier described as love-ness, a physical sensation of subtle intensity, now occurred fairly frequently, and always in connection with people who were in some kind of difficulty. As I was in hospital the incidence of this was more and more frequent; I noticed the difference. The sensation was triggered by an empathetic likeness, and was quite specific, rather like a radar beam picking out a particular kind of object. It was a signal that I had a reason for being there with that person. It would happen regardless of age or sex. And though the feeling was akin to sexual love, it was not actually that. I guessed that empathy had such a reality that it had a physical manifestation. I discovered that it was good to remain detached from this feeling on an emotional level until I was performing my daily yoga asanas, which I had learned to do a year or so because of stiffness in my back. During the asanas I would experience the same glowing sensation and it would flower into a devotion of love and delight, as I have described before, mainly directed to Tom, but equally to Shiva, to Vishnu, to Jesus, to Brahman, and to Buddha, I was aware that sex had taken on a totally different and unique aspect for me. I was in love with God. I was making love – to myself, to him. One could say I was schizophrenic because to do this I had to split myself into two parts, and the one related to the other. But there was as well a whole, a unity. I knew I was in a taboo area but did not feel guilty about it. I didn't have any choice. I had to be that way.

> I've always known the Devil
> The other side of myself,
> Skulking around, like a child
> Playing Bo-Peep
> Always losing things, like sleep;
> A stray cat; slipping in through
> Open windows and doors
> (Who asked *you* to come in?)
> Fated to be chased out, forlorn;
> Get behind, Satan, shadow
> Whatever you call yourself
> Destined for suicide or worse
> Put your head in a bucket twice
> And take it out once ...
> Come, shadow, rest here
> Gently under my foot
> Grow long or short at will
> In the angle of light
> Leap laughing, dance
> Shimmer or shuffle
> Be my friend
> Come in and lick the crumbs

> Falling from this table, mine.
> Widow woman again
> Talking the hind legs and hoofs off
> Taking a human form
> Jack-self, or friend-foe
> Befriend me
> Kiss me
> Judas

I finished the first carving, a curious masculine figure, more tree than man. A sort of totem (or taboo?). I started on another. This was made from the roots of the greengage tree. I upended it, so that the roots would be the hair of the head. It would be a face, a composed face, meditating with eyes open, resting in restful awareness. As I worked my thoughts floated and drifted into the distant spaces, other worlds ...

> Once upon a time, when the galaxy was young and the stars were giving birth, two planets were born to a fiery body called Sun. These delightful twins were destined to circle on an identical orbit, the alter ego of each other; but never to view each other because the intervening space was ever obscured by their radiant father/mother star.
> Through many cycles of time they circled, at first silent and still, enveloped with whirling gases and clouds.
>   But a time came when they were clothed with a garment of green, fragrant and fresh with dew and the rain that fell, gently warm in the rays of light from the great star above.
>   Now it came about that nature, with its infinite manifestations, blessed the twins with living forms of marvellous variety. And these forms developed and flourished through many generations until a full flowering of life was seen in either planet, though different in many respects part of the Earth was warm, and part cold, and here flourished all manner

of wonderful creatures, an abundance of forms, but no sentient conscious ones able to choose their pattern of life

The other orb was called Heaven, and here likewise was a fragrant and fruitful country, and much growth. The planet was inhabited like twin Earth, with living beings, but the path of evolution had taken another route. Here the sentient creatures were built on a different scale with much smaller, lighter bodies in relation to the gravitational field of their planet. One of these could have stood comfortably in the palm of a man's hand, about the size of his thumb. They had a similar body, but with wings, and owing to their lightness and delicacy of structure, could fly to great heights they could communicate with each other, but did so by means of a vibration within the brain. They could also make a wide variety of sounds, but these were more a form of spontaneous expression of feeling, and would be used when the internal vibrations were no longer adequate to convey the meaning of the emotional state of the mind. These sounds were not speech, but music made in the manner of birds. Here also developed activities of all kinds, many artefacts, many structures.

The ease of communication and the benevolent and loving life of these creatures in collective groups enabled them to expand their knowledge of the universe at great speed, and to acquire spontaneously, an immediate capacity to control natural forces, to harness these, and thereby to create remarkable and beautiful forms to enhance their ever-expanding patterns of life. Amongst these were ships that could travel the upper regions of the sky. As the weight of the angels of Heaven was light in relationship to their gravitational field, it was relatively easy to control and power such ships, and quite early in their experiments there were many volunteers to explore the unknown regions. Because of the strength

Fugue

of their telepathic powers, all the angels were at one in their love for each other, and for their beloved Lord, supreme among them, a Supreme Being. He did not always dwell with them, but manifested himself from time to time, sometimes as male, sometimes as female, sometimes as both. When he departed for other worlds, other galaxies, he would leave with his people a clear telepathic communication of love which enabled them to sustain their life without fear, and with an effortless confidence in his return, even though this might not recur for many ages of time.

Angels reincarnated themselves from time to time. They lived in partnership, male and female. When the time came for a renewal, and in order to maintain a variety of forms, the female would lay an egg. This was of metallic substance. The parents would embrace one other, and be instantly consumed by a natural fire, which instantaneously melted the shell of the egg, from which would fly their new bodies, fully fledged and reborn in innocence. A breeze would waft them to a new environment on the planet, each in ignorance of the other's whereabouts until a time of awakened maturity when dominant telepathic powers developed full potential.

Thus Adam and Eve. These two spirits were the most adventurous of the new generation of space travellers. They pleaded with the Lord to be given the commission of flying to the other side of the Sun. They were admonished and told that the time was not ripe, and their experience too limited. Adam and Eve were impatient. They had evolved a concept between them that it would be possible to reach the twin planet Earth, in a new ship they had designed. They were not forbidden to depart but warned that the outcome might be fatal to their status as citizens of Heaven. Angels might not survive as such on Earth. These two were not daunted and made preparations. Finally, before setting out they were solemnly instructed to eat no food from the Earth, but to take sufficient supplies of heavenly fruits and essences to support them until their return.

So the voyagers set forth. The journey itself was charming enough and communications were maintained in the mind as usual, and without difficulty. About three quarters of the distance was completed when the rays of the sun obscured their view of their own planet. Its heavenly beauty had cheered and delighted them for long, with its rainbow coloured atmosphere, a shimmer of light and iridescence. Now Earth came into view, slowly enlarging to the naked eye. A beautiful blue, with drafting and swirling wreaths of vaporous gases surrounding it like a shawl. Adam and Eve were entranced by this first sight of their objective, and felt a curious yearning for it, like that of homing pigeons for their nesting place. Their heavenly thought-partners were aware of this, and again the warning, "Do not eat thereof". Circling the planet at close quarters, passing the moon in its orbit, they were enchanted by glimpses of green, of deep cerulean blue; and made preparations for landing. Down through layers of cloud, blessed with golden light from the Sun, the sky now blue, and this colour more and more alluring to the mind.

A wide circle of sea below, almost to the edge of the orb; the ship descending gracefully without tremor, towards the emerald jewel, an island lying to the upper edge of a great water.

Landing gently, the ship stood silent on a meadow of green turf beside a sea coast facing the setting sun.

It was late afternoon, the sun warm and the summer equinox not long past. "We will call this planet 'Angelland'", they said. And again the curious heartache of homecoming, as if they had been here before.

Food supplies were still ample, the atmosphere of the place excited the explorers' curiosity. Seabirds, white as the clouds, swooped and called around the ship. Adam and Eve were not afraid of these gigantic creatures but regarded them, as all nature, as their helpers and friends. They signalled to one of them, and it landed close to them and sat patiently, watching them with its beady eyes. Both climbed upon its back and nestled themselves deep into its downy feathers, close to the head. The bird spread its wings and flew east and then south. The land spread out below was verdant, a veritable garden. Great lakes reflecting the intense blue of the sky, groves of trees, forests.

Returning they went to their quarters in the ship and made plans. It did not appear that there were other inhabitants in this place. The bird's flight had revealed nothing. No habitations, no clearings or cultivations; just the primeval stillness of trees, grasslands and the quiet movement of an occasional cloud, now passing across the sun. The lingered for a while on the edge of a lake where tiny wavelets broke on a shore of delicate grey sand. Adam and Eve were fascinated by the scale, the size of everything they set eyes on. Trees appeared to them as gigantic sky touching forms, grasses grew above their heads, and they recognised themselves as little' people in contrast to this enormous planet environment. And yet the size of this Earth was the same as their own; this they knew from observing the sun's movements across the sky.

So they settled down to a few weeks of exploration and observation, a blissful time of wonder, when they wandered like delighted children, flying from branch to branch, enjoying the cooperation in flight of many small winged creatures who were obedient to them. And still they kept to their instructions about the food; to eat only from their own supplies. They remained in communication with their parent world and related in thought the beauties of this peaceful place.

One mellow day in the season of fruits, when the bushes and trees were laden with all manner of colourful berries, they set out to follow the course of a river, and eventually rested on the grass at its edge. Eve closed her eyes and listened to her thoughts.

She heard a distant voice very close. Opening her eyes she saw a golden snake coiled in the twigs of the tree.

It was a charming bush, covered with dark, purplish berries, with many clusters, each berry formed of a group of smaller ones. A black berry. The snake was innocently offering her hospitality. "Come", it said, "eat of this fruit – it is sweet and refreshing and will cause you to think many wise thoughts".

Eve was sleepy and not aware of the danger; she impulsively put out her hand and plucked a fruit. Before she had time to recognise her action, it was in her mouth. The taste and texture burst upon her like a flash of light. Her brain was suddenly both cloudy and excited, a heady sensation overpowered everything else in her mind. She turned at once to Adam and placed a fruit in his hand. He read her ecstatic thoughts and took it from her, and he too ate. From this moment both of them were filled with an insatiable desire for the foods of Earth. They began to search for, and eat whatever fruits and seeds they could find, each taste more beguiling than the next.

They forgot all else, and very quickly, before the next moon appeared in the night sky, they forgot that they had come from another planet, only very dimly remembering that it existed and that some kinship remained for them there.

They took themselves out of the ship suddenly feeling it as a cramping enclosed space. They felt cold in the autumn nights and covered themselves and they no longer flew. They found themselves heavy and clumsy – their wings no longer lifted them effortlessly, a dead weight seemed to drag them earthwards.

They had changed; they had grown larger. As weeks passed they grew. The days grew shorter and colder; they were unaccountably afraid. In a last attempt to gain their former status of consciousness and form they decided to take flight. They could scarcely squeeze in the ship. Now more than twice their original size and weight, everything was a confusion of impossibilities, every tool too small to hold and handle, every instrument too tiny to manipulate. And still retaining some vestiges of recall about their scientific, intuitive knowledge, they knew that they could not rise from the Earth in this tiny ship. They had no equipment to make another. They were doomed to exile in this remote place, nevermore to see the Heaven from which they had come. And they wept.

Thus it continued. Each day they craved the foods of Earth, and each day these caused metabolic changes which prevented their return. They became larger and heavier, their bones gradually solidifying, and their minds were clouded over so that the perception of the heavenly world was dim, and they could scarcely hear the inner voice of their Lord, and their angel kindred. Every day came new sorrows, many hazards. Again they wept.

Strange new feelings came, never before experienced. Feelings of loneliness and isolation; then as the winter drew on, cold and hunger also, and with these frustrations, anger and envy; for they blamed each other for this fate, and raged that they could not enjoy the bliss of Heaven, yearning for their lost joys.

Eve gave birth in the spring, but not to herself within an egg. No natural fire came to consume her and her mate. Instead her body split in anguish and from a diaphanous transparent membrane, burst forth two creatures, helpless, half-formed, seemingly blind and without communication. The parents were desperately concerned for these two animal-like recreations of themselves, following a compulsive instinct to preserve their fragile life, seeing it as their own. They were not accustomed to the idea of nurturing an extension of themselves, both rebelled at their own continued existence and the compulsion to remain and nurse the newborn; yet were overwhelmed with love for what, in fact, was themselves in a new unfamiliar form ...

My carving of the head was almost done. A friend liked the face but didn't understand her crown of roots. I explained that my thoughts had been dwelling on the ancient things, Greek legends and such, the old gods of man, of nature, and so I had expressed in form the nature of my Self, as one having roots, roots having outward form, exposed to view – I recognised that my madness was a turning inside out of myself.

Understanding comes subtly, like a long winter dawn in England. We become aware that it is light long after it actually is (the birds start singing before daybreak). My self at the centre, this I know. I'm dimly aware of this and that there must be many patterns, many centres, like the petals on a flower or a spiral form; above all, like a moiré pattern formed by translucent movements in time and space (ours). Centrifugal. When the patterns overlap a new movement is seen; a centrality, or focus just happens, coincidence, or synchronicity. When we become exposed (the black negative film forms a pattern) transparent to black and white, to good and evil, then all things work together for good, because *love* is lord of all. And the root of it is a small domestic detail, like in kind to the little fruit tree growing in the back garden of a middle sized home in a provincial town, An unknown quantity; for this tree, rooted up, axed, sawn, put aside as fruitless and superfluous now is transformed by work, like the wine from the crushed grape, bread from the ground corn; wood subjected to chisel, file and abrasive pressure, steady and persistent. And this Pygmalion, this I, to shape a human worth from discarded material.

Up to this time I had been struggling painfully and laboriously for positive concepts and images. Negative elements in me had been pouring out like puss out of a wound. The crisis were always at times when I was at home and were held and contained by family and friends. I was often afraid and isolated. I felt that my own people could not understand what my mind was doing and that I would never communicate it, never! But, nevertheless, I was *already* learning to do so without quite knowing it. I had begun to write poetry and found in this a natural way to express my newly emerging self.

One Monday morning, early in November, as I started the day's work on my carving, I was suddenly aware of a quiet clearness in my mind. It was as if a window there was wide open. I felt sure, beyond any doubt whatever, that all manner of things would be well and that i (small i) did not have to do, or manipulate anything but just be myself, do what i was doing hopefully, as well as i could, and that i could put aside forever all fear, anxiety and guilt.

> Don't look back or down
> The plank is narrow straight
> One foot and then the other
> Sure balancing, the feat enhanced
> By chance.
> Each follows other in the line,
> "Look, no hands!"
> The trick is – trust.
> We walk together, free, separate Identities, hovering
> on our
> Little strip of life
> Above the immensities of time and space …
> One day waking, we will see
> Amazed, this walking work
> Has width as well
> Planks laid together form the bridge
> Hands reaching sideways in the half-light
> Holding the widening line
> Unending chain of infinite power
> Forever Auld Lang Syne

What I did not realise was that this realization was the merest of beginnings, and that nature's processes of learning had resources of experience in store beyond my liveliest imaginings.

> To Tom – Funnily Enough
> Funnily enough, I do not miss you
> I who am the bow,
> I do not miss the archer and his arm,
> He the beloved
> I do not miss the tree of which I am a leaf
> Though it be hewn
> A rain drop I, yet never miss
> The ocean of thy bliss
> You pulled the bow
> The arrow arches high, flies to the gold
> And never misses it –
> Funnily enough when first you went from me
> I never know that nothing was
> Was amiss
> But though the mist of tears I groped
> Woefully alone, not wise
> Searching for you in every wandering surmise
> It was myself I lost and sought so long
> Who am myself.
> A silence came, beyond the thought of you
> Or of myself
> And thus became myself and also you
> For funnily enough
> Were never two.
> So now I am content to be
> The root or branch or leaf of thee
> For thou and I are one
> The self-same tree

Coda

I give you the end of a golden string:
Only wind it into a ball
It will lead you in at heaven's gate.
Built in Jerusalem's wall.

—William Blake

"**D**on't look back or down," I said. All these words are a looking, and now I was in a different time and place; I was seeing myself and the life I was from that bridge where many planks are set together, and the walking was safe, even the looking back without fear of falling.

Someone made up a story about a boy whose mature self, mysteriously transported from a future time, came back to help him solve a problem and guide him through an adventure where his inexperience could have led to disaster. The boy did not recognise his guide but felt deeply attracted to him; a profound respect and love welled up, obedience also, a sweet, intuitive feeling that flowed easily with no barriers or embarrassments. The relationship was curiously free of the parent-child, teacher-pupil polarity, because the guide, being himself, could in no way condescend or belittle his own growing person at this earlier stage. The helper and the helped were at one, knowing the direction to be correct, trusting every step.

Something like this was taking place.

I left the hospital and began to do the ordinary every-day things, but there was a difference, a feeling that every step was secure, like a climber who knows that his rope is belayed by an experienced leader.

Coda

So much this feeling infused into me that I felt that Tom had come back in just this way – I felt him to be my self returned to find the route with me, not a fantasy this time but a reality. He and I had become a whole person, although funnily enough, it takes two to have a conversation – some capacity in the mind can divide, one to hear and listen, the other speaking in meanings and symbols, instructing and disclosing.

The time came to leave again, move on into yet another pattern of life. The family took the old car down to the sea for a farewell visit; the three boys grown now into young men, and Esther a toddler no more. While they dawdled over the flat rocks and searched for the roundest pebbles, I walked further on to where the rocks were piled up forming a jutting profile. I felt pulled there and quickly lost sight of the others. I climbed higher, so that I could look out over the Severn Estuary, where the light of the evening sun was settling on the grey heaving surface, a tranquil patch, a luminous essence hovering in the immensity. Then I felt whole. A song sang in my mind.

> I went walking down on the rocks
> Beside the surprising Severn Sea
> The white birds flew about my head
> The wandering mind went free
>
> Thoughts came calling for my own true love
> To join my journey on the shore
> He answered me inside my mind
> As he has done before
>
> Two minds with but a single thought
> One pair of feet upon the sand
> Oh when will you come to me my love
> And take me by the hand?
>
> My hands are your hands and your feet are mine
> Our minds nothing can divide
> The rocks may split, the sands may melt,
> But love is ever by your side

> I went walking down on the rocks
> Beside the surprising Severn Sea
> The white birds flew inside my head
> The wandering mind went free.

I sometimes say, "Esther, I had a thought today".
Laughing, she answers, "Mum, what *with!*"

Our minds and bodies correspond to each other, subtly coordinating all the random patterns of response we all must make every moment of our existence. Our consciousness reflects, mirror-like, the state of the whole – body and mind together. Our awareness is the screen, and our activities shape the picture in its movement. One of the paradoxes of consciousness is that if we become aware of the absolute nature of love, we also become aware of responsibility. We feel that intimately. The only possible way to have peace of mind in this condition of life is to transcend, or go beyond, its activity. In the deeply tranquil state of rest we achieve through a technique or process of meditation, the response of body and mind is at-one-ment, integration, we atone for that paradox.

During meditation the metabolic rate reduces to a lower level than it reaches in deep sleep. This produces a very fine type of physical activity which can support the most subtle of perceptions, and leads to a dissolving of tension and the gradual dispersion of accumulated stress.

In this stillness the alert but resting mind can draw together the different levels of consciousness, without effort and without thinking about how this is happening. A sort of lifeline is effected between the extremes of experience. Here I could find a sense of centrality from which I could explore all the areas I had previously found terrifying. Theseus can penetrate the blackness of the labyrinth and emerge from the den of the minotaur through the hazardous tunnels of the great maze because he has Ariadne's thread in his hand. Meditation is such a thread. In nature too, the same symbol is found. A spider perseveringly spins out her thread of connection, trustingly swings out into space, and returns unharmed.

Sometimes I felt that the only guide I had was the meditation itself. It was like having a map in a completely uncharted wilderness. Setting out on a further stage of my journey, I had at last some assurance that it could be successfully completed.

Coda

William Blake said, "Hell is heaven anticipated". This is an accurate, intuitive description of what happens to a manic-depressive. An experience of blissful happiness, energy, joy, occurs on a level for which there as yet is no structure. It is a premature experience of a reality that is potential rather than actual; the actuality has yet to be achieved and won. But the experience, however previous, is real, unforgettable. Like Peter walking on the water, once the moment of ecstatic faith has passed, a feeling of sinking into the abyss is experienced. The structure to support such a state of joy has to be learned, slowly and painfully perhaps, but nevertheless effectively.

The pain of departure from joy is simply a natural process of learning to achieve it. When I began to experience an awareness of this, I was able to fall in with my own deep-level drives towards awareness. The transcending of meditation supported my psyche during the process, constantly refocusing the attention of the mind to its most profound resources, acting as a solvent for blocked stresses and helping the whole organism to act in a way which leads into and with, rather than against a natural flow of self-unfoldment. Just as a climbing rose will produce no flowers if the soil content is not rich enough or it lacks moisture, it nevertheless has the capacity to produce flowers and will do so if conditions are improved by a good gardener. The rose in some way 'knows" that it is a flower-producing organism, and likewise part of the melancholia of the depressive state is that the psyche is aware deep down that the roses are not forthcoming because of a blockage in the supply of nourishment. The meditation I was doing allowed the psyche access to a reservoir of value, through the physical effects of very deep relaxation and rest.

In this way all the experiences which had been for me so far outside the ordinary scope of understanding have become integrated into life-supporting normal activity. No experience is rejected or pushed aside as meaningless; often it means more ... I noticed that some people, many of them meditators, are increasingly aware of synchronicity, a subtle correspondence of events and thoughts; it is expressed in the phrase 'Nature supports'. Baha'i scripture says: "Ye are the fruits of one tree and the leaves of one branch". Our awareness is rippling in the value of our collective mind. Together we grow and evolve, linking our individual awareness to unfold unsuspected qualities: energy of thought to heal the wounded world of its ancient hurts.

At home now I waited, gently, not forcing the pace. I asked for permission to stay on at the hospital as a helper-volunteer, and went each day to the day centre and spent time in the woodwork shop carving both in stone and wood. Esther went happily to a tiny infant school a few yards from the house, Jonas and Joseph were doing 0 levels at the local tech. Very tall and lean they had grown; hair long too, many teenage friends coming and going to the house. The walls shook at intervals as parties gathered themselves under the welcoming roof.

Reuben was in London, his first year at college. When he returned, the proud driver of a motor bike and sidecar, everyone stayed up until dawn and then piled on it for a ride down the dark country lanes to the foot of the Garth Mountain, which was climbed for a view of the sunrise. I left the hospital and got employed as a supply teacher.

The autumn that year couldn't let go of summer; the garden glowed with late flowering yellow sunflowers, the roses renewed themselves again and again.

Many friends of all ages gathered in the big kitchen to drink huge quantities of tea or coffee or wander out to sun themselves in that long-lasting warmth. I felt the glow of it inside too. The warm physical feelings I had experienced earlier continued to blossom, but were not focused on a particular person. I began to notice that people in similar journey or passage situations were naturally drawn together, and my kitchen was as good a place as any for that. I found myself a helper among those needing help. A sharer too.

It became exactly evident that when people gathered in this way, innocently and without, pressure or expectation – a release of energy would be deeply felt by those involved, a strong empathetic joining of hearts and minds. For me this came as a psychosomatic experience. My body felt it too. The feeling of warmth and contact so positive and clear that it completely dissolved negative reactions. Negativity in this context becomes supportive of the positive. The obstacle becomes a stepping stone (the negative film is developed to become a comprehensible picture).

I have felt this connective force with man, woman, and child, old and young, and it affects all of me, body and mind. I am certain that it is engendered by some very subtle kind of vibration, deeper than any perceivable thought pattern, which sets up a link between the psyches of those concerned and thence is transmitted to the nervous system of each.

When this happens, a ripple occurs in the screen of awareness, which is transcendent to the body and mind as such, but includes both in some way. A feeling of at-one-ment comes, and an atmosphere of happiness and validity surrounds each identity.

I could guess that the fact of my own exploring and findings, my acceptance of *all* the areas I found within have enabled me to make links with other minds at a level of being which can connect despite confusion, misunderstanding, anxiety, fear, and all the clutter with which the family and society can surround a hurt mind, and link firmly with an area, which like the profound depth of the ocean, is out of reach of storms, stagnation and pollution where the "true mind admits no impediment". It is what the ancient Indian philosophers call *Ritam Bhara Pragyam* – 'that which recognises only the truth', or in the words of Baha'i scripture: "that Most Great Beauty, through whom truth shall be distinguished from error, and the wisdom of every command shall be tested".

When we moved to Oakwood Road I had no friends close at hand. Esther had no playmates yet, and I began to look around – I watched the people as we passed in the road and often saw one particular mum, a bit younger than me, who had two small daughters and a sparkle in her eye. She would smile and say hello.

I met her in the back lane one day, and gathering boldness, I went up and came out with, "I've seen you often – you live near here, don't you?"

"Yes, at number nine".

"Please come to Esther's birthday – it's a sort of Halloween party. Bring the kids and anyone else you like".

She grinned, agreeing to come. No hesitation at all.

Angela and I had much in common, a friendship from the first moment. We were both art teachers, mums, home-lovers, domesticated. We even looked a little alike.

Very soon I heard her talking about a young married art student, and I quickly realised I had met Julie before when we were both in the local bin. Julie had become pregnant when she was 17 and her parents had insisted she go away to a country hostel and give up the baby for adoption as soon as it was born. Since then she had married and now had two small sons, one only a few months old. Something had gone terribly wrong after the birth of that second baby. Julie would alternatively weep and rage, but more often fall into a desperate prison of silence where no one could reach her. Some immense grief seemed to fill her to the brim, leaving no room for anything outside, even the care of the new baby. Family and friends did what they could, but Julie had retreated to hospital yet again.

Whenever her name was mentioned, there would be a pause and voices would lower. Now even more anguish flared up. Julie had set herself on fire. She had taken a box of matches and put flames all round the bottom of her long Indian cotton dress. The flames had engulfed her in a few seconds, and she was scarred from knee to neck, her very beautiful face unmarked. Now, after five months in hospital where she had arrived almost dead and in a totality of pain, she was physically healed and returned to her home, husband, and children. She could scarcely speak, wept constantly, uttered broken sequences of words in a low voice no one could make out and which seemed meaningless. She sat limply, hands clutched together, eyes downcast.

Angela came round to the house. She sat in the garden and told me about Julie, begged me to go and see her and help if I could.

"They are talking of sending her back to hospital. She is so afraid, so alone. Perhaps there is another way?"

I thought of my own pain, and silently said yes.

Next day I knocked on Julie's door. It was a small terraced house. The place had been recently redecorated by husband, Jim, a young teacher. He looked pale and worried and very tired. As if he had taken all he knew how. His eyes were friendly.

"I don't know what use it will be", he said wearily. "She won't speak to anyone, only to herself – I can't cope".

He finished abruptly, like someone who had a door slammed in his face. The front room was shrouded – the curtains drawn across, the daylight seeped through gently as if not to disturb.

Julie was sitting in a shadow, shrunk into an armchair. She looked small and fragile. I could see the bandages still embalming her throat and wrists, hiding the scarlet tissue of her scars. She did not look up, but I knew that she was intensely aware of our presence. Jim backed away, hesitating.

I nodded and said, 'It will be all right'.

He went, and I turned to Julie. I felt myself quicken, as if a current had been passed through my body. I went up and knelt on the floor, put out both my hands, and took hers. She did not pull them away. She lifted her head.

"I'm Jo, remember? We were in hospital that time".

"Yes", she said. "We are all one person".

Her eyes were grey-blue, very wide apart, and very wide open now. I looked straight into them, and it was like falling into a pool. We held on like that, hands and eyes, for what seemed many minutes.

Then: "I am the Devil!"

"We are both", I replied. I knew about that, the darkness and negation, my own shadow, the vastness of it when the light grew brighter, I knew about the one-ness too, the wholeness that transcends and brings together, that gathers all things.

Jim came back into the room.

"We've got an appointment with the hospital – she doesn't want to go. Will you come with us? She might not mind so much then".

I went back to Julie. "Yes", I said. I gave her my hand again. "If *you* want".

She got up and came to the door, like a lamb to the slaughter. "They won't make me stay, will they?" It was the first thing she had said to us, rather than to herself. Her eyes filled with tears. They flowed silently, and she didn't wipe them away.

We got in Jim's car, and were soon inside the hospital grounds, that same one I had left not so long since. A long slow march down a labyrinth of corridors and into the ward, the strange, familiar feeling of actually belonging here. Julie had been becoming more and more tense; she looked like a trapped bird. She was holding my hand now, very tight, and she walked slowly, as if it hurt her. I sensed anger, and looking at her face saw that it was flushed, lips compressed to whiteness.

She was ushered into the doctor's office by a brusque nurse, and the door was closed. I heard her voice through the glass, 'No!' and again, several times. Then, very quickly she was out, anger flashing strongly now, animating her.

"I won't, *I can't*". She spoke quietly with immense intensity. *"They can't* make *me"*.

Jim went into the office and came out in five minutes.

"It's OK", he said. "The doctor wanted her in, but she doesn't want to take pills, and she doesn't want to be talked to like a child".

I turned to Julie, feeling the pull of her mind. "Why don't you come to my house, stay a day or two? We can talk, and you can sit in the garden, and we can play with Esther and the cat. You can do whatever you feel like. Will you? There's jobs to do there, you could give me a hand".

She did not hesitate. "Yes, Jo, yes".

We arrived at my house and went into the garden. There was a wooden bench there against the back wall and an old wooden table.

I made two big mugs of tea, and we sat sunning ourselves. I did not speak or ask anything. It was quiet and still with the buzzing of roving bees in and out of the sunflowers.

"We *are* all one person!"

"Yes,", I said. "Like the leaves of one tree, all growing together".

Julie looked hard at me. "You are my mother – and your son Jonas is my brother too. I have another at home, and he is called Jonas as well".

She began to talk then, about her childhood, her loss when the baby was taken away, her pain, the flames, and the fear, everything poured out in almost uninterrupted flow.

Esther came home from school. We made supper, and Julie talked on, the tears flowing often, and as quietly as summer rain. I made up a bed for her in my room, and she talked again into the dark.

I think I even fell asleep sometimes but half consciously answered her, and shared with her many of the things that had happened to me – I was able to link into her level of mind and become one with it, and speak to her from there, where she could grasp it best. I told her about the way meditation helps us find our way into stillness and how we could learn to heal our hurts for ourselves, that our awareness could break open any prison of the mind, like a small blade of grass pushing up under the concrete and splitting it to gain the daylight.

Coda

We slept eventually, and I crept out to wake Esther for school. Another day began. Julie talked yet more, and then quite suddenly began to help me with my tasks, simple things like folding the washing from the line, washing dishes, peeling potatoes. We worked together, quiet now.

She said after a while, "I have not done these things for more than a year – it feels good to touch the clean towels and the rough skin of the spuds".

Later, after Esther had come back from school, we all sat in a row on the bench outside. Esther thought Julie was very beautiful and told her all about her dolls, kept bringing her things to look at.

Julie talked back, ordinary little-girl talk, natural and open. Then she said, "I'll go home now".

I phoned Jim and he brought the car.

"Come back whenever you like", I said. "I'll be here".

Two weeks later Julie came to the house, and my Welsh carpenter friend Mog taught her to meditate. Her awareness began to expand from the first moment, and she was able to understand the meaning and value of her growing pains, as I had done, and to see the goal of her life and identity.

A year later she was emerging from her chrysalis of fire, a hopeful, lively, expanding personality. The roots of this quite simply, were friendship and meditation – a sense of kinship. I had an image in my mind of a horizon with the light dawning from beyond its rim. Perhaps it was a symbol of my own recovery – to regain the ordinary world, and yet be aware of a still warmer brightness beyond. I knew something about collective empathy; it had unfolded for the women going down to the beach at dawn, or that long since time when we rejoiced at Tom's 'wake', drawn to unison by love. 'Communitas', someone called it; the anthropology of joy. In nature it happens when a drop of water becomes a snowflake. Suddenly a new form of sparkling clarity and order emerges – a spontaneous fulfilment. A heightened awareness catches, like fire, from one person to another at such moments until all are enlivened, quickened by the same thread or vibration of feeling. As each one moves freely and truthfully in the direction of their own growth, so are their actions and responses appropriate for the others who occupy the same space. Then it is that "all things work together for good for those that love" (God). (This could be one explanation of the experience felt at Pentecost by the friends who loved Jesus of Nazareth.)

The wisdom of the Sanskrit Vedas said it too, three thousand years ago,

> Let us be together
> Let us eat together
> Let us be quickened together
> Let us radiate truth
> Radiate the light of life
> Never shall we denounce anyone
> Never entertain negativity.

Synchronicity – the coming together of people and events (seemingly) by chance, is how we experience the snowflake-like pattern and structure when human minds and hearts are threaded together through a common centre: when *love* is lord of all. When we open the consciousness to the deep areas of awareness we discover the source, fountain-like, of our thoughts, and from which they arise in a continuous flow like bubbles in fermenting wine. I've known that opening, always spontaneously and never through any effort of mine, when loving a person, meditating, praying, listening to some kinds of music. Losing oneself, finding the self.

Sometimes in supremely concentrated action the same things occurs: making a sculpture, running a mile, even in simple domestic tasks like taking the clean washing off the line and folding it, as Julie had done for me that day. Thought bubbles can be comprehended at the deepest levels, before they ever reach the surface. Through meditation, especially, the mind can be settled in quietness and immensely strengthened. Imagine the spokes of a wheel, each one of which is an emerging thought pattern. On the outer rim all possible patterns appear as separate identities, at the hub all converge and are at one. The nearer to the centre the greater is the overlapping of the pattern with another, the nearer each identity to the next ... "A vast similitude interlocks all". As we spiral inward in the dive that a meditating consciousness takes towards the centre, our thought patterns, more and more coincide with those of others. The individual screens of awareness merge and fuse into a space where no thought is – just simple innocence, pure awareness, the source of love. Many people have the experience of spontaneously doing or saying something which precisely matches another person's needs or learning processes – as the saying goes, "Two minds with but a simple thought", synchronicity (coincidence) increases when we are closest to the hub of the wheel.

People like Julie and me, who have suffered a profound shock to the emotional or nervous system, sometimes experience synchronicity in abundance because for a time their range of consciousness is extended, stretched beyond the accustomed span: they touch, in the swinging motions of a shaken mind the outer and inner poles of awareness, from dark to light and back again, from positive to negative, from bliss to despair, making and breaking many connections, never still, lost in a hazardous maze without Ariadne's thread, like to be slain by the minotaur of stress. Julie, dead with disaster, was brought for a moment into the synchrony at the centre, and at that moment her mind grasped the thread.

She knew the centre, "We are all one person". She knew the dark perimeter – "I am the Devil". Now she was beginning to distinguish between the realities and the shadows, just as the light transcends the negative of the exposed film; shining and translucent, impartial, to trust as newly and hopefully as an infant, and yet to be aware, awake, truly alive.

I'd agreed with myself, inner and outer, to go on learning. The next step of this life-school came with surprising swiftness (when would I ever learn?). I had thought myself approaching wholeness and clarity. It all needed trying out; there were some things I had not yet faced, some experiences I would need to encounter and go through; like in old stories there would always be another test.

Esther and I had come back from a camping holiday on the coast of Pembrokeshire. We had walked in the scented heather and grass of the headlands, watched the seals at play in the surging waves below, sunned ourselves, breathed in the sweet air blowing from the Irish Sea, sat by the leaping campfire and watched the sparks fly up to the stars, hugging our mugs.

Two women who were learning and growing, like me, began again out of a wasteland of loss. Three daughters between us, and a bright-eyed dog to run on the sand and splash with us into the spray. We would meditate together after a day on the beach, and there was a joining of spirits.

No sooner back in Oakwood Road than another sequence began. Just as an invitation had come from America, so another came now to begin a new style of life, an unexpected and unfamiliar task. Joseph's girlfriend, Rachel, came to see me. This 17-year-old had become a second daughter, spending more time in our home than in her own family's so that she could go to the comprehensive school of her choice, rather than to the one nearer her mother's house.

Her intelligent eyes glowed. She looked very determined. "I want you to talk to my mother and Tim – they have something important to ask you".

Rachel was the elder daughter of a widow named Andrea, who lived with Tim, a man some twenty years younger. They had met as students at the local university. Andrea had struggled with enormous loss; of husband, of a newborn baby, and of her health. Tim was a lifeline to a new confidence. Both had a streak of adventurousness, and this had blossomed into an idea: to set up a shop which would sell all kinds of beautiful things from other countries than Europe. They would travel abroad to find them and needed someone to manage the shop. They had a Land Rover and a lot of imagination, but no funds.

I agreed to go into partnership with them, a compelling impulse that could not be denied. Within weeks I had sold my house to carpenter Mog so that he could establish a school of meditation. I used the proceeds to lease an old shop premises in the High Street of a cathedral city where many tourists and pilgrims came. It would be a grand exercise in sharing and living together. As I packed my household into boxes I wondered if I had enough energy and stamina for what seemed an enormous task. Andrea had a young daughter of 9, Esther's age, and an 11-year-old son. With Rachel and Joseph that made eight of us. We would somehow have to squeeze into the upper floor over the shop, a very tiny space for so many people. Andrea and Tim planned to leave for India to find beautiful things for the shop after a few months of setting up the business, so there would be more space in due time.

We all experienced the stress of overcrowding, intensified by our own differences in outlook and personality. Tensions, hopes and fears, anger and reconciliation flared up and down. There was the joy of work, and the weariness; I did not see how I would manage on my own when Tim's family left for India. I became very afraid. The weeks went by, and I became more and more uneasy. It felt as if I was on a moving belt which was carrying me towards an abyss. Rachel and Joseph felt it too. But for them there would have been no shop, nevertheless the undercurrent of tension became too much; they quarrelled and misunderstood each other. Joseph suddenly left for London where he got a bed-sitter and started a lonely life working at some A levels. Then one January day the Land Rover set off, loaded high, as if never to return. As I waved them farewell, I felt like Atlas, with the world on my back, although it was only a small shop.

When we bought the place it had been a small conventional restaurant which sold bread and pastries. We had continued with that and sold some Oriental crafts and clothes at the back of the shop as well. An odd assortment. The bread arrived at six thirty each morning, there were dishes to prepare the night before, accounts to do, and helpers to organise. I was unsure of how to manage and integrate all these things; I felt caged in.

Within weeks it was clear that we could not make ends meet. I saw the accountant, and he urged me to recall my partners, saying that their help would be needed to sort things out. In an agony of decision I sent a telegram to Turkey, where they had arrived. I had to face failure then and come to terms with it, accept the fact of it. I could do nothing else. Tim and Andrea drove their loaded Land Rover back across a freezing Europe, and when they arrived their anger was a fiery furnace, and I was cast into it. They felt betrayed and cheated. All the plans had come to nothing.

"How could you do this to us?" Andrea shouted bitterly, surveying the litter of unpacked boxes that had come out of the Land Rover. "We will never forgive you, never".

I was obliterated. Before I had lost a husband, I had lost balance of mind, now I was losing self-esteem. Or was it just my ego? I was losing a sense of proportion as well. I blamed my partners for what was happening to me, I defended my deflation by becoming self-righteous and opinionated. I was right and they were wrong. It didn't come out well and it got worse. Only one thing could ease everyone. I moved out. We agreed that I would be freed from shop duties to attend a training course to become a teacher of meditation. When I returned, Esther and I found lodgings, and I came into the shop every day to work. We toiled hard at recovering the business and gradually things got into shape. There was a hesitating reconciliation. Joseph came back from London with two A levels and almost at once both Rachel and her mother found they were pregnant.

Meanwhile, I was making another kind of beginning. I became a Baha'i. Nobody I knew had ever heard of this, nor had I until I met this idea in the form of a young family who used our restaurant regularly. I had been attracted to them at first meeting by an atmosphere of serenity and tolerance which they radiated, and I was not surprised when Tony and Ann explained that they got their value of life from a spiritual teaching about unity, one-ness. Oneness of God, of religion, of mankind. That made sense to me. My heartaches had all come from lack of it. They evaluated some things not as political but as spiritual truths – equality of men and women, the relinquishing of all prejudice – to look for value in a person, always, and leave aside the negativity, never being offended by it, or seeking to put down or devalue another human being.

This was very near the bone of my present troubles. I decided to throw in my lot with this idea, and began tentatively to practice it. I had responded mainly to what I thought were the faults of my workmates, thinking myself in some way better. We freely exchanged our negative impulses, never stopping to think where they were coming from. Now I resolved to make the attempt at least, of submitting to the free natural flow of my feelings, to let the impact of another person's words pass through the mind without being stopped, mauled around, reasoned upon. Not merely to ignore as 'in one ear and out the other', but to hear the message without the stress that comes with it, to sift out the content without making a value judgement about the person. "The power you

Coda

have to hurt or belittle me, I give to you". My concern, if I could manage it, would be with groceries, not the grocer, with the content of the friend's comments, not with the friend, with the food and not with the cook. An idea could be allowed to pass through the mind without being stopped and hurled back with a charge of rancour, ridicule or defamation. Thus I could become grateful for whatever would come my way, because without new experience, even including failure, ridicule and frustration, I cannot develop new strengths and skills.

As this concept of life took hold of my imagination, I had yet another bridge to cross. This was equally unfamiliar. Several times that autumn I had fallen sick; a blinding headache, vomiting, and weakness would knock me onto my bed. I recovered and was again as sick as a dog. My temperature soared in the evenings and my body seemed in revolt. A series of red, swollen patches appeared in unpredictable places, here and there without apparent cause. Then I noticed a small pea-shaped swelling in my groin. It began to grow – it swelled daily and looked more and more menacing until it was several inches long and a lurid purple. Walking became painful. My doctor could not decide what was wrong. Antibiotics were ineffective. I began to think I had cancer. I knew I was ill in a way I had never been before, that I would possibly die if I could not get help. The day Andrea gave birth to a daughter I was at the brink of despair. I went to another doctor, and he got me into hospital, an intensive care ward where two at least were dying. Esther was welcomed back to the shop, where she would stay safely while it was decided what my fate would be.

I lay back on the high bed and thought about death. It was Christmas Eve. Early that morning a woman had died. They pulled the curtains all around the other beds. I had thought the nurses were just washing the other patients. While I waited my turn I decided to clean out my handbag. I emptied the contents onto the bed, and just as I had finished and was shaking the bag upside down over the waste-bin to remove the last dregs of dust and small particles, I saw the low trolley sliding past, the long grey box just visible below the drawn curtains.

"So that's it", I thought. That body we think so much of – it's just a bag, and will be thrown away as so much rubbish. I felt myself step over a threshold. There was a certitude, a dimension of trust which was overwhelming and all-embracing. I wept, feeling an immense gratitude. A nurse came and held my hand. She didn't ask me why I cried, she simply stayed a few minutes, accepting me.

Later that morning the surgeon came and examined me. "You're going to be fine, Mrs Thomas. All you have is a TB gland. We'll drain it, and you'll have lots of streptomycin and those huge pills you may have heard about – big as horse pills, they are!"

The certitude stayed on. Eight weeks is not so long, after all, and I am writing now. Every day I fill the pages and hours. People in here die sometimes. It seems all wrong to me, that the dying are not trusted to have much awareness of the value of that transition. They are not respected.

"Yes, dear, you'll feel better in the morning".

And yet another life-support gadget is applied. That most valid of processes is set aside, covered up, hushed away. Everyone pretends it doesn't happen. A woman in the next bed, her eyes wide with astonishment and disbelief, dies for the one and only time, shocked out of her mind by the fact that she doesn't understand what is happening. I vowed that one day I would work to make it different. Tom's death had validated me, brought me nearer some truth. Mine, when it came should do the same. I would leave a legacy of truth for my heirs. Death would be an enormous leap of growth into spiritual value, a messenger of joy. I would share that joy, and growing further on I would leave a spark of growth behind for others to use. Another kind of thread, like the one Tom had given me.

So to begin. Everyone accepts scientific truth – the roundness of the earth, the structure of atoms, the laws of entropy. Spiritual truths are less readily accepted. For a Baha'i, as indeed for the Christian, and other faiths, physical death is to the soul as the broken mirror is to the sun. The sun continues to shine even when the rays are not reflected in the mirror. Like the sun, the soul is undying and continues its evolution. My journey is forever, and there will be many arrivals, like the pulse of the seasons, the life cycle of the stars. All endings will prove to be a beginning, as Tom Elliot had said.

Released from hospital, I drove the old car down into the town, feeling like a school kid on the first day of the holidays. I had a visit to make, to another hospital. Rachel and Joseph's newborn baby looked up at me from her mother's arms, her eyes wide, oceanic. They had called her Sophie, which means wisdom. My first grandchild. It was a beginning for us both, and for Rachel and Joseph too, newly formed as parents. That was a big act of creation, I thought, to make parents, grandparents, aunts, and uncles all in one go. Clever kid. I made up a song for her, to sing with my Welsh harp. A journey song.

 I went back to work in the shop with a hopeful heart. While I was in hospital, Tim found me a spacious house at a cheap rent. I moved in with Esther and some student friends to share. One of them, Ellen, began to be very tense, even angry. I quickly found out why. I was still only a part-time housewife, not keeping things really tidy and clean, although I made gestures in that direction. I had learned something by a bitter route that long since time when I had been turned out of my lodging by my landlady. Now it was a lodger who complained, the same anger coming from a different direction. I had often grumbled that our shop was not tidy enough. Now it was my turn to be on the receiving end. I accepted the need to change something and got to work on it. Ellen's anger flared up from time to time when the dishes got piled up in the sink, or the gas stove was left greasy. Her standards were exacting, but I learned fast. We were sharing a home, and I knew I must gather new habits and skills. As they developed, so did friendship. The atmosphere relaxed, changed.

 A year later we gave a joint party to all our friends, a celebration of shared work and value. We put up an old frame tent of Tim's, decked it out with colourful Oriental rugs and wall hangings, lots of bright cushions, the Christmas tree lights to see by, and candles too. It was a fine summer night and we had baked bread. The fragrance of it wafted through the house, making a welcome. Rachel came over to help with Sophie in her pram. The house glowed and the candles twinkled. The whole family turned up, and many more. Not least my co-granny, Andrea, her large shoulders draped in a magnificent embroidered caftan. We never spoke about that slowly healing anguish, but the warmth flooded into the embrace, and both hearts knew that wholeness and trust were in sight at last.

 Now it was that I discovered beyond any doubt that I would never stop learning.

This life, this exchange we all make, giving and taking, moving or staying, is evolution. We all grow together when we grow.

It's eleven years since Julie came to stay, and this learning and growing are as active as ever. I begin to notice that a change has come over my "emotional" life. I find myself less confined to exchanges with one particular kind of person 'my kind'. It seems that the person I am *with* is the most important person at any moment of time. That human being will be worth every ounce of my attention, and I will give to him or her a maximum value if I can, totally validate that person, even if outward appearances belie or belittle that value.

My training as a teacher of meditation had showed me a way to respond to other human beings regardless of the amount of stress they might be carrying or reflect in their behaviour, their lifestyle, culture, or creed. We could synchronize our thought patterns and find the value at the source of thought, at the centre, flow over the obstacles of stress to the roots of our awareness, effortlessly. Meditation was the nourishment at root level, its effect deep within, silent, unseen. The other side of the coin is following a faith: a spiritual teaching was the turning of the growing structure of life to the light, as leaves turn to the sun. There two things perfectly complemented each other.

Rueben, Jonas, and Joseph found direction now as grown men, and before long I was a grandmother again. Esther and I were a lively partnership when the boys had left and we learned to trust, even more as her natural flow towards independence took her into explorations of her own. Someone told me about a job. A worker was needed to run a hostel for people coming out of psychiatric hospitals, or maybe needing refuge from destructive happenings at home. I applied, and presented myself for an interview at the MIND office.

I found myself confronted by four very pleasant older ladies, social workers, and the like. I didn't try to conceal anything about myself but told them plainly about my times in the bin.

"I feel that's my greatest asset". I went on. "It's the hair of the dog that bit me: I'm not afraid of mental illness, or of myself".

They gave me the job, and I worked for two years, made a lot of friends as people came and went. Some were able to grasp the thread

Coda

and come out of the labyrinth as Julie had done. Some grasped and then let go. They wander still, but the thread is there for the taking.

My kinsfolk tell me I'm a nomad.

My tent was pitched on yet another site when I found myself invited to join a university course to become a social worker.

A late starter, like Tom, I became a student at age 55. It was as he had often said, good to be given time to read, write, think, and learn. A chance to explore and exchange a wealth of insights and make even more connections. Two years more, and once again I prepare to enter hospital; this time as a worker. I shall need a lot of thread.

The day is just awake. Soft light, half light as the neon burners dim to a dull orange and go out. Milk bottles clink into the shadowy doorways as the milk-men run, rubber shod, from float to open gate, soft padding on the pavement. My feet too, as I jog, filling my lungs with good clean air before the morning traffic pollutes it. The lights turn red and I jog across, onto the footpath under the trees, beside the grass where early questing seagulls rest, joined by a thin white mist shrouding the green. One foot and then the other, easily, no strain, breathing even and unforced.

Granny round the park and its six thirty on a summer morning. The grass has been cut under the trees, a sweetish smell, and the air is not cold. I pass a middle-aged man wearing an old hat, walking his middle-aged dogs. He is there most days and calls good morning. The dogs smile too and run alongside for a few paces until he calls them back. I'm round the first side of the huge recreational field. While the feet move the mind moves too, or stays still, like a buoy on the top of the waves which appear to move steadily along. Another jogger passes me, a young man running at twice the pace – I beckon him on like an overtaking sports model. Next comes a man off to work on his push-bike, riding alongside for a few yards. He shouts, "Hup! Hup!"

I call back, "Why don't you try it? It's good for the heart!" I start a prayer in my head, words following the breath – the rhythm of my thudding feet. "I love the love of God in my soul, and I love the love of God in the soul of Gill". (or Ann, Lyle or Amy....)

I name my friends in this way until I reach my door again. I'm sweating, refreshed, relaxed: ready for a meditation.

As I drift into silence I hear, the words of Baha'u'llah* coming from the deepest place to the ear of the mind. "Ye are the leaves of one tree and the fruits of one branch". (Yes, Julie, we are all parts of one organism, one person.)

---

* (1817–1892, Founder of Baha'i faith)

Rest

*T*ime out of Mind ... the rest is yet to come. Rest from the running and striving, but not from the endeavour to make and become my self in the next stage of evolving reality.

I have discovered, at last in my tenth decade that I do not need to try, to strain after this unfolding self, but as the Beatles sang it ... *let it be.*

Afterthoughts

If I'd heard of a different framework of ideas about human consciousness and perception, and had access to some alternative concepts about our relationship with the divine – God, or source of our being, or whatever name our respective tradition uses, I might have been less exposed to the fear and confusion of the experiences I have recorded, for which I was totally unprepared …

Here are some of the ideas and words that helped to remove the misunderstandings which had triggered many of my extreme responses.

Our Relationship with God

In Hindu scriptures, Upanishads declares "He is far and He is near. He is within all and He is outside all". In the Old Testament we read that God said, "Let us make man in our own Image". In the New Testament, Christ says, "I am in the Father, and the Father in me. Neither shall they say, 'Lo here! or, lo there! for, behold, the kingdom of God is within you'."

In the Qur'án, God says, "Man is my mystery and I am his". In the Baha'i Writings we learn that God says, "Thy heart is My home; purify it for My descent. Thy spirit is My place of revelation; cleanse it for My manifestation. And also in your own selves: will ye not, then, behold the signs of God? And be ye not like those who forget God, and whom He hath therefore caused to forget their own selves. In this connection, He who is the eternal King hath spoken: 'He hath known God who hath known himself'".

Nevertheless, the whole *is* greater than the parts. Our imagination can only picture that which we are ourselves able to create. Generations of humans have imagined God as a man, something we easily understand.

Afterthoughts

But there is more: "I testify that thou wast a hidden treasure wrapped within thine immemorial Being and an impenetrable mystery enshrined in thine own essence. Wishing to reveal thyself, Thou didst call into being the Greater and Lesser worlds, and didst choose Man above all thy creatures, and didst make Him a sign of both of these worlds". (Baha'ullah)

The lesser worlds ... from which emerges in due time from the mineral (inorganic); vegetable (growth): animal (movement): humans (consciousness/awareness, intellect), nearest in creation to the Divine, to the nature of God.

These divine qualities in a human being: How do they become part of human nature, rather than in the animal world?

The essence of these qualities is 'pre-existence'. A place of pure undifferentiated potentiality, an unmanifest source. Think of the sun. Its energy radiates heat and light through the emanation of its rays. It radiates; and this radiant energy translates itself on our planet Earth in a myriad life forms, and abundance. Likewise the spiritual sun, the essence of spirit, has its own emanating rays; we call this the "Holy Spirit", and this animates all things and is the life-giver. The sun itself does not descend and become its own light waves! Just as an artist or craftsman who has just completed a marvellous painting cannot become the paint on the canvas. The painting is an emanation of the painter's vision and skill. The writer does not become the pages of the book he is writing, and the pages have no comprehension whatever of the writer. The carpenter is incomprehensible to the beautiful table he has made. We all issue from the energy source which is the primal energy of God, and we do not comprehend it, although we are *of* it.

The law of opposites applies to the world of comprehension, it's how we experience. Hot/cold, up/down, inside/outside; all our knowing is based on this. We experience darkness as absence of light, and the opposite effects on us of fire and light. The absolute has no opposite, no counterpart. The realm of creation is not in this category: the Creator remains in essence of singleness; has no need of the existence of any other being or thing.

"There is no doubt then, that of all created beings man is the nearest to the nature of God, and therefore receives a greater gift of the Divine

Bounty". the Baha'i Writings thus describe the ultimate emanation of the Divine spirit.

In His book The Hidden Words, Baha'u'llah makes this abundantly clear; He gives voice to the Word of God, thus … …

"O son of utterance! Thou art my stronghold; enter therein that thou mayest abide in safety. My love is in thee, know it, that thou mayest find me near unto thee.

O son of being!

Thou art my lamp and my light is in thee. Get thou from it thy radiance and seek none other than me. For I have created thee rich and have bountifully shed my favour upon thee

O son of being!

With the hands of power I made thee and with the fingers of strength I created thee; and within thee have I placed the essence of my light. Be thou content with it and seek naught else, for my work is perfect and my command is binding. Question it not, nor have a doubt thereof.

O son of man!

Thou art my dominion and my dominion perisheth not; wherefore fearest thou thy perishing? Thou art my light and my light shall never be extinguished; why dost thou dread extinction? Thou art my glory and my glory fadeth not; thou art my robe and my robe shall never be outworn. Abide then in thy love for me, that thou mayest find me in the realm of glory.

O son of spirit!

I created thee rich, why dost thou bring thyself down to poverty? Noble I made thee, wherewith dost thou abase thyself? Out of the essence of knowledge I gave thee being, why seekest thou enlightenment from anyone beside Me? Out of the clay of love I moulded thee, how dost thou busy thyself with another? Turn thy sight unto thyself, that thou mayest find Me standing within thee, mighty, powerful and self-subsisting.

O son of the throne!

Thy hearing is my hearing, hear thou therewith. Thy sight is my sight, do thou see therewith, that in thine inmost soul thou mayest testify unto my exalted sanctity, and I within myself may bear witness unto an exalted station for thee."

Afterthoughts

So it is abundantly clear that we do not seek for our relationship with the Spirit of God, out there; outside our own presence, our self; we look inside. And the portal for this is stillness, silence; all growing things in the realms of being, of nature, grow from inside to outside. No exceptions. In silence we come closer to oneness, the divine core of ourselves and all others. Then we may be aware of *"The still, small voice"* that speaks in the silence and we have in our human nature a paradox – the animal/human, spiritual/divine are all present in each one of us. *"A human being stands at the end of night and the beginning of day"*. We have the capacity to choose which direction – towards the godly side of ourselves, the spiritual/positive, or towards the animal/physical.

People are inclined to say "How can God allow all the misery and suffering in the world?"

All the negativity, the dark side, are the result of human choices; *our* choices.

Natural disasters? It may well be said we helped create those too, because of our disastrous exploitation of the planet's resources for our own greed. The laws of cause and effect are deep and complex, but one day we will learn to support and nurture the planet that is our life-giving source.

The human being, emanation of the divine spirit is always yearning for perfection, to find this better way, step by step, learning, changing, growing. Each arriving heralds a new stage of the journey. There is always a further level of this growth.

As the poet TS Eliot described it:

> We shall not cease from exploration
> And the end of all our exploring
> Will be to arrive where we started
> And know the place for the first time.

We can choose to explore, to awaken, to strive, and with all our strength to reach for the next stage of ourselves. And it may well be that this is simply to be aware, know ourselves above all else, as spiritual beings.

"Whatever is in the heavens and whatever is on the earth is a direct evidence of the revelation within it of the attributes and names of God, inasmuch as within every atom are enshrined the signs that bear eloquent testimony to the revelation of that Most Great Light. Methinks, but for the potency of that revelation, no being could ever exist. How resplendent the luminaries of knowledge that shine in an atom, and whatever is in the heavens and whatever is on the earth is a direct evidence of how vast the oceans of wisdom that surge within a drop! To a supreme degree is this true of man, who, among all created things, hath been invested with the robe of such gifts, and hath been singled out for the glory of such distinction. For in him are potentially revealed all the attributes and names of God to a degree that no other created being hath excelled or surpassed. All these names and attributes are applicable to him. Even as He hath said "Man is My mystery, and I am his mystery".

Even as He hath revealed: "We will surely show them Our signs in the world and within themselves". Again He saith: "And also in your own selves: will ye not, then, behold the signs of God?" And yet again He revealeth: "And be ye not like those who forget God, and whom He hath therefore caused to forget their own selves".

In this connection, He who is the eternal King – may the souls of all that dwell within the mystic tabernacle be a sacrifice unto Him – hath spoken: "He hath known God who hath known himself".

From that which hath been said it becometh evident that all things, in their inmost reality, testify to the revelation of the names and attributes of God within them. Each according to its capacity, indicateth, and is expressive of, the knowledge of God. So potent and universal is this revelation, that it hath encompassed all things visible and invisible"

(Gleanings from the Writings of Baha'u'llah)

*Out of the fusion of two souls
a third subtle entity is born;
though invisible and intangible on earth
it is the composite souls of two lovers.
The progress of one mysteriously influences the other.
They become the tutors of each other's souls.
Distance or death,
mere physical forces
cannot cause its disintegration.*
—'Abdu'l-Bahá

156
130 things
128 light
121 Seq. of thoughts effect on the environment.
114 looked of a reality of a sound of fantasy.
99 Jung more friends in subconscious
84 Back in time —
80 Something spoke at the back of my head.
76 Being in love w God.
66 Electro therapy
57 Vally in love in Universe —
34 Dream / I had been in heaven
   Bells in my head.
5 Observing myself —